A COMMUNITY
OF EXILES

═══ Michael Goonan, SSP ═══

A COMMUNITY
OF EXILES

Exploring
Australian Spirituality

ST PAULS

Acknowledgments:
Scripture quotations taken from the *New Revised Standard Version Bible,* © copyright 1989 by the Division of Christian Education of the National Council of Churches of Christ in the United States of America. Used by permission.
Extracts from *Cloudstreet,* by Tim Winton, © copyright 1991, McPhee Gribble, Ringwood, Australia. Used by permission.
Extracts from *Woman of the Inner Sea,* by Thomas Keneally, © copyright 1993, Hodder Headline, Australia. Used by permission.

A COMMUNITY OF EXILES:
exploring Australian spirituality
© Michael Goonan ssp, 1996

First Published, September 1996

National Library of Australia
Cataloguing-in-Publication Data:
Goonan, Michael
A community of exiles: exploring Australian spirituality
ISBN 1 875570 78 0
Bibliography
1. Spirituality – Australia. 2. Religion and culture – Australia.
3. Australia – Religious life and customs. 4. Australia – Exiles – History.
I Title.
291.40994

Cover photo: *Coorong sand dunes, South Australia* – Northside Photographics/CD Watkins

Published by
ST PAULS PUBLICATIONS – Society of St Paul
60-70 Broughton Rd – (PO Box 230) – Homebush, NSW 2140

ST PAULS PUBLICATIONS ————————————————
is an activity of the Priests and Brothers of the Society of Paul who proclaim the Gospel through the media of social communication.

Contents

Foreword

The idea for this work arose during my first semester of studies at the Graduate Theological Union, Berkeley USA. In the early part of 1988 I was struck by the similarity of themes that were emerging in two of the courses I was taking. "Post Exilic Literature" with John Endres SJ, and "Tragedy and Redemption in Modern Literature" with David Batstone I saw how the ancient writers and the modern writers were grappling with similar issues – tragedy, guilt, exile, abandonment and, in the midst of it all, redemption. These are the issues of human beings of all ages, including myself. I wished to explore them further in my Master's thesis and I felt that a good way to do this would be to put the biblical texts and the modern novels in dialogue.

David Batstone introduced me to the two Australian novels that became the basis for this study and I grate-fully acknowledge his considerable formative influence on this work.

John Endres agreed to coordinate my thesis committee and gave direction to my study of the biblical texts. I thank John, and the other members of my committee Antoine Moran SJ, who guided my study of the literary texts, and Elizabeth Liebert SNJM, who enriched the project with her background in Christian spirituality.

Nancy Thompson, RD, read the texts and the various drafts of my thesis and engaged me in many critical discussions on them. Her insights, interest and encouragement are much appreciated. I thank also Bula Maddison for many helpful insights.

Foreword

The idea for this work arose during my first semester of studies at the Graduate Theological Union, Berkeley, USA, in the early part of 1993. I was struck by the similarity of themes that were emerging in two of the courses I was taking: "Post Exilic Literature" with John Endres SJ, and "Tragedy and Redemption in Modern Literature" with David Batstone. I saw how the ancient writers and the modern writers were grappling with similar issues – tragedy, guilt, exile, abandonment and, in the midst of it all, redemption. These are the issues of human beings of all ages, including myself. I wished to explore them further in my Master's thesis, and I felt that a good way to do this would be to put the biblical texts and the modern novels in dialogue.

David Batstone introduced me to the two Australian novels that became the basis for this study and I gratefully acknowledge his considerable formative influence on this work.

John Endres agreed to coordinate my thesis committee and gave direction to my study of the biblical texts. I thank John, and the other members of my committee: Annette Moran CSJ, who guided my study of the literary texts, and Elizabeth Liebert SNJM, who enriched the project with her background in Christian spirituality.

Nancy Thompson, MD, read the texts and the various drafts of my thesis, and engaged me in many critical discussions on them. Her insights, interest and encouragement are much appreciated. I thank also Bula Maddison for many helpful insights.

Brian Grenier CFC, tracked down numerous articles on the novels in Australian publications. Without the help of someone in Australia it would have been impossible to write this work in the United States. I thank Brian, Margaret Commins RSM, Nestor Candado SSP, Nerina Zanardo FSP, Peter Malone MSC and Rita Ruzzene SGBP for reading the thesis on my return to Australia and offering valuable pre-publication comments.

My two and a half years in Berkeley were an especially rich time in my life. It was a time of voluntary exile from Australia which gave tangible expression to an unnamed but felt sense of exile within my own being. My growing sense of being at home in the land of my exile mirrored my journey towards the discovery and claiming of a home place within myself. I am grateful to the many people who companioned me so lovingly during my time of exile in the United States.

I appreciate that it was the personal and practical support of the members of my religious community, the Australian Region of the Society of St Paul, that made possible this time of study, renewal and growth. I am grateful to them, and to the members of my family and many others, who since have welcomed back this returning exile with great warmth and have supported me patiently during my time of re-entry. I hope that through this book, and in other ways, I can share some of the riches of my exile journey.

Introduction

Exploring Australian Spirituality

For the past twenty five years, many Australians have been exploring theology in a local context. They have been considering how the distinct, if not always unique, Australian experience influences the way we investigate, understand and express our religious belief.

Underlying this inquiry is a recognition that human experience is a primary source of divine revelation. The task of theology is not to dictate or determine experience, but to help individuals and communities to understand and evaluate their experiences, to help them see the presence and activity of God in their lives.[1]

Since human experiences occur within particular cultures, and are affected by the race, gender, education and social position of the people involved, it is appropriate for specific theologies to emerge out of particular places and cultural experiences.

The muddy waters of human experience also provide a starting point for much contemporary spirituality, concerned as it is with the integration of all aspects of human life. As experiences differ from place to place, distinctive spiritualities are also emerging within particular places and cultures. Through this book I hope to contribute to the exploration of Australian spirituality.

When we talk about the experience of Australians, we cannot forget that white settlement in Australia began as a community of exiles. Between 1787 and 1868 the British Government transported one hundred and sixty thousand men, women and children in bondage from England and Ireland to Australia.

The years following the Second World War witnessed the arrival in Australia of another wave of exiles from Eastern and Western Europe, people who had been forced to leave their homelands by famine, unemployment, lack of opportunity and the devastation of war. The past twenty five years have witnessed another wave of refugees to Australia, this time from Asia, victims of war and political oppression.

A particular tragedy throughout is that the first wave of exiles in particular, and their descendants, managed to exile many of the Aboriginal people from their own family groupings and from their sacred sites and tribal areas, from the core of their spirituality and way of life.

Studies in Australian spirituality need to take into account the original experience of exile, and the continuing effects of exile on Australia's present population. Exile is not the only determining characteristic of Australian spirituality, but it is a significant characteristic and one that I will explore in this book.

The title of this work, *A Community of Exiles*, contains an obvious contradiction. Community suggests connectedness and belonging, while exile speaks of forced separation from all that is dear, of estrangement and alienation. However, the thesis of this work is that healing, growth and redemption are possible for Australians of all races and ethnic backgrounds if they are able to live within a community that can acknowledge the painful shared experience of exile that is at its heart.

The spirituality outlined in this book will hopefully speak to Australians. Because of the shared aspects of human experience, it may speak to others as well. I will be delighted if people can say of this work what Robert

L. Ross, of the University of Texas, said of Tim Winton's Australian novel *Cloudstreet.*[2]

> *Cloudstreet* is an ambitious work and most often an admirable one that depicts not only the Australian experience of seeking "community" but also that same endless quest of people everywhere.[3]

A literary approach

I will explore the contemporary Australian experience of exile by examining two recent Australian novels, *Cloudstreet*, by Tim Winton, and *Woman of the Inner Sea*, by Thomas Keneally.[4] A prior reading of these novels will be helpful for understanding the present work. However, those who have not read the novels should not be deterred from reading this book. I will give some outline of the plots where this seems necessary to make my comments intelligible.

I will also adopt a comparative approach to the study of exile. I will study the experience of the Jewish people who were exiled from Jerusalem by the Babylonians in 587 BCE, to see what light this experience can shed on the Australian experience of exile. Maintaining a literary approach I will explore the Jewish experience of exile through the biblical short stories of *Tobit* and Hebrew *Esther.*[5]

The four texts to be studied have been carefully chosen. The books of *Tobit* and *Esther* reveal quite diverse responses to the experience of exile. The same can be said for the two Australian novels. *Tobit* and *Esther* were composed some two hundred to four hundred years after the Babylonian exile.[6] They are thus addressed to descendants of the original exile generation who are still living with the consequences of that traumatic event. The same applies to the two novels which describe the experience of contemporary Australians.

A connection also exists between the biblical books and the Australian novels. The plots of *Tobit* and *Cloudstreet* bear striking similarities. Both stories involve two families in distress. We thus have a double plot, with two tensions that gradually intertwine and become one. In both stories a marriage unites the families and contributes significantly to the resolution. The characters in each story are guided by an angel – Raphael in *Tobit* and "a black angel" in Cloudstreet.[7] Both stories also highlight the importance of family for survival in exile. But they are family stories with wider implications. By staying together despite difficulties, these families offer models for survival for the larger exile community.

Similarities also exist between *Esther* and *Woman of the Inner Sea*. In both stories the hero is a woman threatened by the power of evil men. Lacking material or political might, she must rely on her personal resources – inner strength, wisdom, courage, cunning, beauty – to survive the crisis and conquer evil. Both women are Queens. Esther is the wife of the Persian King, Ahasuerus, while the woman of the inner sea, Kate Gaffney-Kozinski, is called the Queen of Sorrows.

Neither woman chooses her role, but both find they are called to it. The call in both cases is mediated by an older male relative, Esther's cousin, Mordecai, who adopted her at birth, and Kate's uncle, the not-so-Reverend Frank. Both men are ambiguous characters who, paradoxically, bring guidance and consternation to the hero.

Unlike the family oriented stories of *Tobit* and *Cloudstreet*, in *Esther* and *Woman of the Inner Sea* we witness an individual called upon to face a crisis situation. In these latter stories, however, it is precisely the actions of the individual that bring healing to the exile community and ensure its survival.

The diversity of response that we find in the biblical stories, and again in the Australian novels, together with the similarities of plot between the biblical stories and the novels, make them ideal texts to set in dialogue.

To interpret and understand these texts I will follow the approach outlined by Hans-Georg Gadamer and described by Sandra M. Schneiders in her important work, *The Revelatory Text*.[8] This approach involves a dialogical process of questioning the text, receiving an answer and questioning further. Gadamer maintains that every text is an answer to a question about something. One cannot understand the answer that the text constitutes until one understands the question to which it is the answer.[9]

One can ask the text other questions and receive fruitful answers. I will be asking each of these texts: what can you tell me about exile and the spirituality which flows from it?

I will explore the literary techniques utilised by the authors to communicate their message. This is very appropriate for the study of the novels but also for the biblical stories. In recent decades there has been an upswell of interest in the Bible as literature. As Robert Alter has noted, literary art plays a crucial role in the shaping of biblical narrative. To appreciate the theological implications of these works we must pay attention to:

the minute choice of words and reported details, the pace of narration, the small movements of dialogue and a whole network of ramified interconnections in the text.[10]

Besides examining the authors' literary techniques I will, where appropriate, provide some historical background to the texts and utilise some other sources that help to explain them.

It is valuable to bring the insights of the biblical texts to our study of the modern novels. I believe that the Bible, which records the "experiences of persons and communities witnessing to the transformative power of God in their lives,"[11] is an authentic source of divine revelation and an important referent for people's present day experiences. As Philip Sheldrake has noted, theologies and spiritualities need "particular religious and doctrinal referents"[12] in relation to which they can be evaluated and clarified. The Bible is a primary referent. To determine the validity of a particular spirituality one needs to ask, among other questions: is it consistent with biblical revelation? As Schneiders notes, this question is complicated because the biblical text contains historical inaccuracies, scientific errors, mythological assumptions that make no sense to the modern mind, and even morally objectionable positions.[13] There must, therefore, be an ongoing critical dialogue with the biblical text about its subject matter. However, provided this is done, I believe the stories of *Esther* and *Tobit* do provide a valuable referent for evaluating the experiences and spiritualities described in the novels.[14]

The purpose of studying the experience of exile in these four texts is to help delineate an Australian spirituality. Sheldrake has correctly noted that "spirituality is one of those subjects whose meaning everyone claims to know until they have to define it."[15] We must, therefore, conclude this introductory section by offering a definition of the term 'spirituality' as it will be used in this book.

A definition of spirituality

Recognising that human experience is a primary source of revelation, I will adopt an anthropological approach to spirituality.[16] This approach argues that spirituality is an element in human nature and experience. It is a reality intrinsic to human persons as such[17] namely that dimension whereby they are able to grow as persons through their life experiences. While some people find their negative life experiences overwhelming and ultimately destructive, others not only survive such experiences but emerge from them as persons of greater wholeness able to know the truth, to relate to others more lovingly and to commit themselves more freely to persons and ideals.[18]

Integral to this growth process is an experience of self-transcendence in which people find their lives integrated or made whole in relation to some reality greater than themselves. Overcoming any tendency to self-preoccupation, they are able to remove their own ego from centre stage and put some Other there. Accordingly, Sandra Schneiders has proposed that:

> the primary application of the term spirituality is to that dimension of the human subject in virtue of which the person is capable of self-transcending integration in relation to the Ultimate, whatever that Ultimate is for the person in question.[19]

The anthropological approach to spirituality is human, inclusive and experiential. It emphasises that "every human being has a capacity for spirituality or is a spiritual being."[20] It is not merely concerned with exceptional private religious experiences but with "every area of human experience, the public and the social, the painful, negative, even pathological ways of the mind, the moral and relational world."[21] The study of spirituality in this anthropological approach is cross-cultural, inter-religious and interdisciplinary.[22] Its first concern is to survey and describe the complex mystery of human growth, before moving to analysis, criticism and construction of new possibilities.[23]

In this anthropological approach we can speak of human spirituality, religious spirituality and Christian spirituality. Human spirituality is the capacity for self-transcendence in every person. When this capacity for self-transcendence is actualised in relation to the Holy, however this is conceived, we have religious spirituality. When the Holy is experienced as "God in Jesus, the Christ, by the gift of the Spirit"[24] we can speak of Christian spirituality. The integral connection of human, religious and Christian spirituality must be emphasised. Since the Christian, for instance, comes to know God in Christ only through the experience and the symbols inseparable from human community and history, Christian spirituality must include every dimension of human life. Christian spiritual development is intimately connected with total human development.

Following Walter Principe we must also note that the term spirituality is applied to three distinct levels.[25] First, there is the real or existential level. Here spirituality refers to the capacity within human beings for self-transcending integration and the actualisation of that capacity. This is the level of raw human experience. At the second level spirituality refers to the formulation of a teaching about the lived reality. The authors of the biblical texts and the novels that we will study in this thesis provide a spirituality at this second level. They are not simply providing raw human experience but in writing their stories they have consciously selected and ordered that experience to provide a spirituality of exile. At a third level, spirituality refers to the study of the first and especially the second level by scholars. This is the task I am undertaking in this book – a study of the spirituality of exile formulated by Tim Winton and Thomas Keneally, and by the authors of *Esther* and *Tobit*.

Following the anthropological approach, I will take for my starting point the lived, particular experience of the characters portrayed in the texts. I will first seek to describe the experience of exile and the spirituality that is expressed in these texts. Only after having described the experience will I attempt, in the final part of this book, to interpret the texts.

I will now enter into dialogue with these texts to see what they have to say about the experience of exile and the spirituality which derives from it. I will begin by exploring an ancient experience of exile, that of the Jewish people living in the Diaspora.

PART ONE

AN ANCIENT EXPERIENCE
OF EXILE:
LIVING IN THE DIASPORA

1

Exiled to Babylon

In 587 BCE the Babylonians, under King Nebuchadnezzar, overran Jerusalem and destroyed its Temple. They then marched the Jewish king, the artisans, the priests and the prophets, indeed all of Jerusalem's leading citizens into exile in Babylon, some eight hundred miles away, forcing them to live as refugees, oppressed and separated from their homeland.

The initial conditions in which the exiles were detained in Babylon are practically undocumented. But it appears that they were kept together in compact groups settled on deserted agricultural sites.[26] Whatever their actual physical conditions, they were profoundly affected by the traumatic events. Their grief at losing their homeland was great and the crisis was deeply spiritual. Their sense of abandonment by God was acutely felt. The grief they experienced is well expressed by the psalmist:

> *By the rivers of Babylon*
> *we sat mourning and weeping*
> *as we remembered Zion.*[27]

It appears, however, that these exiled Jews did not remain in their detention camps for long. At some stage the camps were dissolved and the exiles were permitted to make their way in more open society. Some enlisted in the Babylonian government service and many became a part of the cosmopolitan population of the city of Babylon prior to its conquest by the Persians in 539 BCE. Lester Grabbe notes that a large and thriving Jewish community arose in Babylon.[28] With the accession of the Persians further opportunities for advancement came. Consequently, when the Persian ruler, Cyrus, permitted displaced peoples to return to their homelands the vast majority of Jews in Babylon chose to stay where they were. Only a minority, a remnant, dribbled back to Judah.

Not only were the Jews comfortably settled in their new environment but a return to Judah was unattractive for many reasons. First, the Jews who had stayed in Palestine, did not particularly want the exiles back. For many of the "poor people of the land"[29] who had not been exiled, life had improved somewhat when the leading citizens had been taken into exile. With the departure of their landlords many who had been tenants came into land of their own. Rivalries and clashes occurred between the returnees and the resident population, tensions which were often explained in religious terms but in all probability were largely socio-economic in origin.[30] The socio-economic unattrac-tiveness of a return was increased by the fact that Judah's borders had shrunk during the period of the Babylonian exile. Territorial encroachments by neigh-bouring peoples had left a greatly reduced heartland in Judah. Much fertile land had been lost. Finally, Judah remained under foreign rule. The Jews were not returning to a situation where they could resume full control of their destiny. For all of these reasons the task of restoration was going to be extremely difficult. A return to Judah was an unattractive proposition for many Jews in Babylon.

We must also note that the Babylonian captivity was only one phase of a larger dispersion of Jews that had begun as early as the Assyrian destruction of the Northern Kingdom in 722 BCE and which accelerated greatly during the Persian and Greek periods.[31] The uncertainties and inequities of life in Palestine coupled with the socio-economic attractions of the wider world meant that many Palestinian Jews chose to leave their homeland in search of a better life. Jewish communities were established in many parts of the ancient Near East. These communities came to be known as communities of the Dispersion, or the *Diaspora*, as distinct from the continuing community in Palestine.

Because a return of exiles to Judah after 539 BCE was possible, though arduous and undesirable, and because many Diaspora Jews were not originally exiles or the descendants of exiles, it can be claimed that after 539 BCE Jews living in the Diaspora were not a people in exile.

That is a correct judgment from an historical point of view, and it possibly represents the felt experience of many Jews living in the Diaspora. However, many Diaspora Jews continued to experience themselves as being in exile. This was certainly the case with the Diaspora communities for which the stories of *Esther* and *Tobit* were originally composed. As I will demonstrate, these stories are true exile stories. We can, at this stage, note the narrators' immediate concern to link their principal characters with exile. In *Esther* the Jew, Mordecai, is introduced as a descendant of Kish who "had been carried away with King Jeconiah of Judah, whom King Nebuchadnezzar of Babylon had carried away."[32] As Esther is Mordecai's cousin she is also a descendant of exiles. Likewise Tobit's first affirmation of himself is that he is an exile, taken into captivity by the Assyrians.[33] His relative Sarah speaks of herself as living "in the land of my exile."[34]

Second, the setting for both stories is a precarious situation in which the survival of the Jewish people is severely threatened. This is reflective of an exile situation where one is subject to foreign powers. Ironically, both stories highlight that exile existence can be both precarious and prosperous!

Most importantly, as I will show, the questions that gave rise to the stories are exile questions. Will Soll has noted that all of the evils that happen in *Tobit* – loss of place, property, respect and community solidarity – "are shown to be acute manifestations of a more chronic problem, the exile itself."[35] The same can be said of *Esther*. The Jewish people's initial plight is directly related to their status as a landless people subject to a foreign power – a people in exile.

I will now dialogue with these texts, exploring the questions which gave rise to the stories and examining the answers they provide.

2

Where is God in all this?

Walter Brueggemann and John Donahue have said that while the exile crisis had many dimensions, the Jewish people knew that finally it "must be faced in terms of God, God's freedom and God's faithfulness, God's power and inclination."[36]

For the Jewish people the ultimate question raised by the exile was the God question: has God abandoned the Jewish people in exile? Closely related is the issue of *theodicy*: does God permit the righteous to suffer and the wicked to prosper? The exile experience brought these questions into sharp relief for the Jewish people. They had to find satisfactory answers if they were to maintain their religious identity which was at the heart of their broader cultural identity.

Underlying the stories of *Tobit* and *Esther* is the fundamental question of exile: is God faithful or absent?

The authors of both stories acknowledge the felt experience of the absence of God. Far from denying it, they highlight it in their stories by employing a technique of *concealment*. In the Hebrew text of *Esther*, God is truly concealed. God never appears or speaks, and the divine name is never uttered. The narrator also conceals other facts from the reader. He never explains why the Jew, Mordecai, refused to bow to Haman, the senior official in the Persian court,[37] even though this action provokes the whole crisis of the story. Nor does he reveal why Queen Vashti, the original wife of the Persian king, refused to display her beauty before the guests at theking's banquet, a stance which brought about her demise.[38] We can speculate about the reasons but the text gives no definitive answers. The narrator also suggests that concealment is appropriate at certain times: it is acceptable for Esther to conceal her Jewish identity while in the King's harem[39] and to conceal her motive for inviting the King and Haman to the two banquets.[40] The narrator is saying that concealment is indeed necessary to ensure the survival of the Jewish people. The inference is that there are good reasons for God to conceal God's presence from the Jews at this time.

The concealment theme is also very pronounced in *Tobit*. Tobit's blindness symbolises the inability of the Jews in exile to see God. Tobit conceals from his wife Anna that he has prayed for death which is why he has sent their son, Tobias, on a journey to recover Tobit's money. He doesn't answer her question, "Why is it that you have sent my child away?"[41] In turn the major secret of the story is concealed from Tobit. He actually mentions it, "a good angel will accompany [Tobias],"[42] but he has no idea he is speaking the literal truth. The identity of the angel, Raphael, the messenger of God, is deliberately concealed until the action of the story is completed. Only then does Raphael say:

> I will now declare the whole truth to you and will conceal nothing from you. Already I have declared it to you when I said, "It is good to conceal the secret of a king, but to reveal with due honor the secrets of God."[43]

Raphael then explains the reason for the concealment: "to test you."[44]

Thus while the narrators of both stories acknowledge the exile experience of an absent God, they stress that God is not truly absent. Rather God's activity is concealed from the Jews at this time for good reasons.

Indeed, both narrators stress that the concealed God is truly active on behalf of the Jewish people.

The author of E*sther* does this most forcefully by utilising the technique of peripety, the sudden and unexpected reversal of fortunes, a technique that is often found in folk literature. As Sandra Beth Berg has noted, a study of *Esther's* "literary structure demonstrates that events conform to a peripatetic principle." [45] The reversals of fortune apply not only to coincidences in the story but are built into the structure of the narrative which provides a symmetrical series of theses and antitheses, situations and reversals. Until 4:12 everything is going badly for the Jewish people. In 4:13-16 Esther decides to risk her life for her people. From that moment the peripatetic principle becomes apparent and, through a remarkable series of coincidences, fortunes reverse. All that was threatened on the Jews in the first half of the book redound on their enemies in the second half. Was this reversal of fortunes mere chance, or was it God's plan? The consciously structured pattern of the book suggests the latter, that God is firmly in control of events. It is significant that this unexpected reversal of events occurs only after Esther assumes the initiative and acts to save her people. We will take up this important point in the next chapter.

The narrator of *Tobit* is far less subtle in emphasising that God, though concealed, is acting on behalf of the Jewish people. The author uses the technique of the *omniscient narrator* who quickly shares his[46] omniscience with the reader. In 3:16-17, immediately after the hapless Tobit and Sarah have prayed for death, the narrator says:

> *At that very moment, the prayers of both of them were heard in the glorious presence of God. So Raphael was*

> *sent to heal both of them: Tobit, by removing the white films*
> *from his eyes, so that he might see God's light with his eyes;*
> *and Sarah, daughter of Raguel, by giving her in marriage to*
> *Tobias, son of Tobit, and by setting her free from the wicked*
> *demon, Asmodeus.*

The omniscient narrator clearly emphasises that while the characters cannot see God, God is acting on their behalf and all will work out well. The narrator removes the suspense from the story. We, the readers, can sit back and observe the action from above.[47] Our question is not "Will God help them?", but "How will God help them?" We can enjoy the action and smile at ironical comments such as Tobit's assurance to his wife, Anna, on their son's departure on a difficult journey:

> *A good angel will accompany him; for his journey will be*
> *successful and he will come back in good health.*[48]

We, but not Tobit, know just how true his words are! The narrator of *Esther* allows his readers no such release of suspense.

Both stories, therefore, stress that God, though concealed, is active among the people in exile. However, it is interesting to note that the books conceive of God's presence differently. In *Esther* God is portrayed as very immanent, working in and through the actions of the Jewish people. God is inextricably with the people in exile. In the later work of *Tobit*, a much more transcendent God is portrayed, a God who communicates with the people through intermediaries such as the angel Raphael. There is a sense of a God who cares for the people but is spatially separate from them. Raphael has to be sent to Tobit and Sarah, suggesting spatial distance. Sarah prays "with arms outstretched towards the window"[49] which the original readers would have understood as facing Jerusalem.[50] *Tobit*, which looks to a glorious restoration of Jerusalem and the Temple, does have a sense of the fully restored Temple as being the place of the presence of God. The story does, however, reveal a God who is wholly interested in the Jews in exile.[51]

This brings us to the issue of *theodicy*. Both stories affirm that, despite appearances, ultimately the good will prosper and the wicked will be punished for their evil deeds.

Esther has often been condemned for its bloodthirsty final section in which the Jews destroy their enemies.[52] In the eyes of the narrator, this bloodletting was necessary. It is not enough for the good to triumph; the wicked must also be punished for their evil deeds. Retribution must be seen to happen. The narrator is keen to emphasise that this was just retribution. People who were not hostile to the Jews were in no danger. The Jews attacked only "those who hated them".[54] Their response is excessive but in the context of the story it is necessary to balance the excessive response of Haman to Mordecai's refusal to bow before him. In the decree formulated by Haman all Jews were to be destroyed, killed and annihilated and their goods plundered.[55] Such an excessive decree could only be balanced by another permitting Jews to destroy, kill and annihilate their enemies and to plunder their goods.[56] The narrator stresses that the Jews did not, in fact, exact full retribution. Despite the decree's permission, they did not plunder the goods of their enemies.

The book of *Tobit* also brings the issue of theodicy into sharp relief. In the autobiographical opening section Tobit affirms that:

> *I, Tobit, walked in the ways of truth and righteousness all the days of my life.*[57]

He then enumerates his acts of charity to his fellow Jews and his faithful observance of the Law. Like Job, he is an innocent man suffering "undeserved insults".[58] Observing his condition, his wife, Anna, verbalises the issue of theodicy: "Where are your acts of charity? Where are your righteous deeds?"[59] In other words, what good has your fidelity to God brought you? This rebuke prompts *Tobit's* prayer of lament in which he pleads for death. That prayer, coupled with the lament of another innocent sufferer, Sarah, is heard by God who sends Raphael to bring healing and reversal of fortune to them both. Theodicy is once again upheld. In this book also it is not enough for the good to prosper. The wicked must also suffer. In the final verse of the story Tobias hears of the destruction of Nineveh and the deportation of its citizens into Media:

> *Tobias praised God for all that he had done to the people of Nineveh and Assyria; before he died he rejoiced over Nineveh, and he blessed the Lord God forever and ever. Amen.*[60]

Not only have the just prospered, but the wicked have received their just desserts.

We must note, however, the eschatological character of both stories. The just will triumph and the wicked will perish...eventually! The narrators of both stories are addressing Diaspora Jews who are leading a difficult and precarious existence in an alien environment. In the face of such a distressing situation these people are wondering whether it is possible or even desirable to cling to their distinctive heritage.[61] The narrators' basic appeal to them is to remain faithful to their Jewish heritage during this crisis. George Nickelsburg has correctly noted that:

The story of Tobit's suffering and its alleviation is paralleled by the story of Israel's suffering and its alleviation. But whereas the healing of Tobit (and Sarah) brings closure to that plot, the story of Israel's suffering remains unfinished. From the time perspective of the alleged author and from the point of view of the real author, God's mercy on Israel will be realised in the future. Tobit's story, with its happy conclusion, is the paradigm of Israel's story, which remains to be concluded.[62]

The narrator's exhortation to the Jews in exile is expressed in the words of Raphael to Tobit: "Take courage; the time is near for God to heal you: take courage."[63]

Likewise, in *Esther*, the narrator is urging his readers to be patient. There is no need to panic in the face of difficult circumstances. By stripping the story of all non-essential details the author has created "a fast-paced suspenseful tale."[64] As we read the story we feel events are happening too quickly. The couriers speedily dispatch the King's decree;[65] the day of destruction of the Jews seems to be fast approaching. In this way the narrator intensifies the feeling of suspense and panic. But in reality the story is unfolding slowly. It begins with the King spending 180 days banqueting[66] – there is no haste. The process of preparing and selecting a new queen to replace Queen Vashti takes four years:[67] again, no haste. And there are eleven months between the royal edict's promulgation and the day of destruction of the Jews. There is time to do something. Esther can afford to execute her plan slowly and carefully over a number of meetings with the King. She can always wait another day. The slow time line of the story is the narrator's way of telling his readers to be patient and persistent in their efforts to remain faithful in difficult circumstances. There is no need to panic. The Jews will triumph and their enemies will be punished eventually. But it will not happen overnight.

So both narrators set their stories in a past historical time and have a significant orientation towards the future, but their focus is on God's presence now in the lives of the people. As Nickelsburg has written concerning Tobit:

> [T]he author of *Tobit* focuses on the presence and activity of God's healing angel *here and now*. Raphael's mission is placed neither in primordial times nor in the eschaton; it is in historical time that he descends to heal the suffering of human beings....Although the book of Tobit is set in past time, its characters are real human beings with whom the readers can identify. The implication is that God is now present among his people, and God's angels are active to heal the ills of God's people.[68]

We have seen that the authors of *Tobit* and *Esther* both grapple with the essential question of exile: Where is God in all this? Both respond that God, though concealed, is presently acting on behalf of the people. Both affirm that eventually the just will triumph and the wicked be punished. Patience is needed but, as we shall now see, so also is action on the part of the Jews in exile.

3

What must the Jews do in exile?

The narrators of *Esther* and *Tobit* both stress that God's involvement in the life of exiled Jews always stands in creative tension with human responsibility. The survival of these communities rests not only with God, but with both God and the Jews themselves.[69] While the key question underlying both texts is the God question, closely related to it is the question of human responsibility: What must the Jews do in exile? In fact, with regard to *Esther*, it can be argued that this is the central question. By completely concealing God's presence in the story, never mentioning the divine name or divine activity, the narrator is consciously putting the emphasis on human activity. He is not anxious about God's activity. He knows God will do God's part. He is concerned about the peoples' activity. He ends the book not by praising God but by praising Mordecai who "sought the good of his people and interceded for the welfare of all his descendants."[70] The narrator also stresses that the unexpected reversal of events happens only after Esther assumes responsibility and acts to save her people.

The narrator of *Esther* thus emphasises the importance of *human initiative and daring* if the Jews are to survive in exile. As a weak and powerless people in a foreign land they must put to use all of their personal skills if they are to survive: cunning, patient planning, skilful speech, concealment of identity, even physical beauty. All of the qualities of the wise person, as outlined in the wisdom tradition, need to be utilised.

In all of this, the major quality required of Jews in exile is *a principled adaptability*. This is essential for people who live in subordination in a foreign land. To survive they have to be able to go with the situation, to work within it, while remaining faithful to the essential elements of their tradition.

The great model of adaptability in the story is Esther. She offers a model for living in exile and is the true hero of the book which is rightly named after her. In contrast, her older relative, Mordecai, finds it difficult to adapt to changing circumstances and as such he is not a good model for exile living. The narrator is very sympathetic to Mordecai and speaks well of him, but he makes it quite clear that it is the intransigence of Mordecai, his refusal to bow to Haman, that precipitates the crisis for the Jews.

When Esther first appears in the story she is subservient to her relative, Mordecai. The narrator notes that, "Esther obeyed Mordecai just as when she was brought up by him."[71] In the King's harem, however, she adapts to the new situation and shows more initiative. In the harem she "won the favour" of Hegai, the eunuch in charge.[72] The phrase "won the favour of" is active in meaning.[73] She consciously takes steps to put herself in the best possible position. Later, when Esther, who is now Queen, learns about the crisis facing the Jews, she adapts to the situation once again and decides to act on behalf of her fellow Jews. Risking not only her status as Queen but also her life, she assumes the central role in the crisis. In 4:17 the narrator notes that Mordecai "did all that Esther commanded him". From that moment Esther is the initiator. The helpless Mordecai can do nothing but wait and hope that her efforts will be fruitful.

Having assumed the initiative, Esther's character comes to full flower as she skilfully and courageously puts into effect her plan to save the Jews. In her careful planning and wise speech, she emerges as the sage in the wisdom tradition. Esther's ability to adapt to changing circumstances, to find new resources within herself to face new crises, offers a key to survival in difficult situations. As Andre LaCocque has noted, Esther is "the harbinger of an astonishingly adaptive Judaism that lasts until this day."[74] Sidnie Ann White has noted that in her ability to negotiate skilfully a difficult course, Esther "is a model for the successful conduct of life in the often uncertain world of the Diaspora."[75]

White further suggests that Esther's being a woman helped her to adapt to life in the Diaspora. There the Jews were the powerless, subordinate members of society. This is precisely the position women frequently experience. During centuries as subordinate partners they have developed survival techniques. In exile they, and not the men, had within themselves the resources to survive and grow in a situation of subordination. Thus not only Esther, but women in general, were models for living in the Diaspora.[76] This theme will re-emerge in our study of the Australian novels where women again come to the fore in exile situations.

Tobit also places great emphasis on human activity. However, the emphasis is not on human cunning and inventiveness but on religious activity, the observance of the precepts of the Mosaic Torah. The narrator highlights Tobit's faithfulness in keeping the precepts of the Law: he observes Jewish dietary laws;[77] he follows the law about ablutions after becoming ritually unclean through contact with a corpse;[78] and he follows the example of the *Genesis* patriarchs in commanding Tobias to marry a woman from his own tribe.[79] The importance of right actions with regards to one's family and tribe are also emphasised: duties towards one's parents, the obligation to bury the dead and the importance of using one's wealth responsibly for the benefit of others. All of these activities are subject to divine reward and punishment.

Especially significant is the emphasis in *Tobit* on *almsgiving*. In this story we are dealing with wealthy families. Despite having his property confiscated, Tobit appears to be relatively prosperous after his return from hiding and he has a vast amount of money in safe keeping in Media.[80] The responsibility of such prosperous Jews to care for their less advantaged kinsfolk is a central message of the book. Almsgiving is rewarded by God. It "saves from death and purges away every sin. Those who give alms will enjoy a good life."[81]

Finally we must note the great emphasis the author of *Tobit* places on the activity of *prayer*. Every major turning point in the story is punctuated by prayer. In 3:16-17 the narrator notes that it is precisely in response to their prayer that God acts to heal Tobit and Sarah. In the story specific types of prayer are illustrated. In their plight Tobit and Sarah pray the prayer of *lament*.[82] This is an especially suitable prayer in a time of distress, when one needs to articulate grief before a God who is both king and enemy.[83] The story reveals that healing comes, sometimes in the most unexpected ways, when one verbalises grief in lament. On their wedding night Tobias and Sarah utter a prayer of *petition*.[84] In response to good fortune, all of the characters utter hymns of *thanksgiving*, *blessing* and *praise* of God.[85]

4

How should the Jews relate to their gentile overlords?

Jews in exile also have duties towards the gentiles among whom they live. Not only must they declare to all people the deeds of God, they must also be good citizens in the land of their exile. A very important question underlying both stories is how should Jews in exile relate to their gentile overlords?

This is a pressing concern for the narrator of *Esther*. He displays no interest in a return of the exiles to Judah. Despite the difficulties involved, remaining where they are offers the best guarantee for Jewish survival. Accordingly, he argues that it is possible to be both a good Jew and a good member of the Persian empire. The two identities are compatible, indeed intimately related.

First, the best way for Jews to promote their own well being is to serve the empire well, as Mordecai and Esther do. Only a foolish king would take the lives of good citizens. Second, by being a good Jew and working to save her people Esther also promotes the well being of the empire which is enriched by the contribution of the Jewish people. David Daube has noted that the narrator of *Esther* had possible gentile readers in mind as well as Jewish.[86] He argues that the book has a political purpose of demonstrating the valuable contribution Jews make to the empire. At a most basic level, the Jews help the empire financially through the taxes they pay. Haman knows the King will have to be financially compensated for the destruction of the Jews so he offers the king an immense bribe, "ten thousand talents of silver",[87] for the life of the Jews.

Also, in the story the only people who have the King's best interests at heart are the Jews. It is the Jew, Mordecai, who saves the King from an assassination plot.[88]

The narrator also seeks to allay general fears about the Jews as being separate and different from other peoples.[89] He places little emphasis on distinctive Jewish practices. The story displays no interest in Jerusalem and its temple cult, or in Jewish practices of piety. The narrator shows no concern with upholding Jewish dietary laws. Esther can eat what she likes in the harem. The narrator is also comfortable with inter-marriage between Jews and gentiles. I believe one reason for not emphasising distinctive Jewish practices is to reassure gentiles that Jews are not so different and do not need to be viewed with suspicion.[90] The narrator's point for the Jews is that they can be both good Jews and good members of the Persian empire, and his exhortation to them is to be both. This obviously involves living a certain tension, as LaCocque has well expressed:

> They must bear two names and two faces; have two calendars and two agendas, don two sets of clothing, eat at two tables, hold two discourses, live at the edge of two worlds.[91]

This is not easy to do. Wisdom is required. At times it will be wise to conceal one's Jewish identity; at times it will be propitious to reveal it. But do not resolve the tension by ceasing to be a Jew or ceasing to be a good member of the empire. The narrator's message is clear: as difficult as it is, live the tension; it is in your interests for survival, and also in the best interests of the state.[92]

The narrator of *Tobit* also stresses that Jews are not bad members of the state. Tobit notes that in the early days of exile he served the Assyrian King, Shalmaneser, well. He appears to have held an important office in the Assyrian court:

> *I used to buy everything he (Shalmaneser) needed. Until his death I used to go into Media and buy for him there.*[93]

Also noteworthy are the gentile influences in the story of *Tobit*. Aspects of the heroic fairy tale, common in many traditions in the ancient world, are found in this work.[94] Scholars, in fact, suggest that two ancient folktales, "The Grateful Dead" and "The Monster in the Bridal Chamber", provide the structure for the plot.[95] Ahiqar, an ancient wisdom hero who appears in many traditions, also makes an appearance in this book where he is portrayed as a relative of Tobit. Also significant is the connection of *Tobit* with the broader wisdom tradition. This tradition began as an international intellectual movement which transcended cultural and even religious boundaries.[96] It was concerned with the proper ways to govern one's life, even one's nation, so that success and tranquillity would be assured. The origins of the wisdom tradition are in the family and the tribe.[97] Fathers, or clan leaders, would pass on to the next generation the lessons they had learned about life. The family wisdom tradition is well represented in the fourth chapter of *Tobit*, where Tobit gives his son instructions, not just for the journey ahead, but for life. From its family origins the wisdom tradition moved to the royal courts. This influence is also present in *Tobit*, where Tobit and Ahiqar are portrayed as being members of the court. It is, of course, also very apparent in *Esther*.

Many non-Jewish influences are, therefore, discernible in *Tobit*, a broadening of outlook that happens in exile. We must note, however, that ultimately *Tobit* is a Jewish sacred book shaped not only by secular influences and the broader wisdom tradition, but principally by the Deuteronomic reform, the prophetic tradition, and the specifically Jewish wisdom tradition in which wisdom is equated with Torah. What emerges is a Jewish religious book which, unlike *Esther*, places great emphasis on the distinctiveness of Jews and gentiles. The narrator opposes intermarriage with gentiles,[98] calls for full observance of the Torah and looks to Jerusalem as the Holy City.[99] The Jews are in exile to witness to the greatness of the God of Israel: "Acknowledge him before the nations, O children of Israel; for he has scattered you among them."[100] As Craghan writes:

> [T]he author's message is clear: dare to be different. He urges them not to conform to pagan practices but to translate the heritage of Israel into day by day covenant living. To be a covenant people means to be different.[101]

The books of *Tobit* and *Esther* are, therefore, quite different in their approach to the gentile world, with *Esther* playing down differences between Jews and gentiles and *Tobit* emphasising distinctiveness. It must, however, be noted that the focus of each story is different. In the words of LaCocque, the concern of *Esther* is "to show the face of the Jew that is turned towards the world."[102] In *Tobit* the focus is the other way around. What is presented is the Jewish face in exile turned towards Jerusalem. Consequently, the stories consider different issues. *Esther* is concerned with relations between the Jews and the state, and argues that the best chance for Jewish survival lies in the right exercise of Jewish influence within secular government. *Tobit* is concerned with the Jewish family in exile, and argues that the best chance for survival lies in faithfulness to the Torah and the purity of the family. Because the focuses of *Esther* and *Tobit* are so different we cannot draw the facile conclusion that these stories are in opposition on the relationship between Jews and the gentile state. It is quite possible that the author of *Esther* would have considered intermarriage among Jews and certain Jewish religious practices to be desirable or at least necessary in some cases. Likewise, the author of *Tobit* would have probably agreed that it is important for Jewish officials at court to work for the well-being of Jews. We should not force these texts to answer questions the authors are not asking.

A more valid question is perhaps to ask: why is the focus different? I believe that at least part of the answer is connected with the final question we need to ask these texts: Do they envisage a journey of return? The answer in *Tobit* is definitely yes. The narrator sees the Jews' time in exile as temporary and this, I believe, leads him to emphasise distinctiveness and ethnic purity. The narrator of *Esther* does not envisage a geographic return. That being the case, he argues that the Jews must learn to get along with, and live fruitfully in, the gentile state. We must now investigate more deeply this question of whether, and how, the narrators envisage a journey of return.

5

Is a journey of return envisaged?

As previously noted, concealment is a key literary device adopted by the narrators of both *Esther* and *Tobit*. Indeed, I believe the best way to capture the narrators' principal concerns in these stories is to consider what they most conceal. Thus in *Esther* the author totally conceals the presence and activity of God in order to stress the importance of human activity and initiative. His primary concern is to stress that humans must act.

The narrator of *Tobit* is even more surprising. By use of the omniscient narrator who reveals all to the reader he creates the impression that he is telling us everything. But in fact he conceals the central message of his story until the final two chapters. When Tobias is reunited with his parents and shows them his new wife, Sarah, and the identity of Raphael is revealed, the family tale has ended. All that remains to be said is that "they lived happily ever after." But at that moment the author reveals the hidden meaning of the story. The misfortune and reproach experienced by Tobit and Sarah and their glorious deliverance from that misfortune is a prophetic symbol of the suffering and deliverance of the Jews from exile. And it is something more: it is a symbol of the suffering and restoration of Jerusalem. The narrator reveals that this is his primary message not only through the use of concealment but also through repetition. He makes the point first through Tobit's hymn of praise in chapter thirteen and then through the narrative discourse of chapter fourteen.

Tobit is committed to the Deuteronomic reform with its insistence that the Jerusalem Temple is the only place where Israel may lawfully worship the Lord.[103] The narrator is aware of the Temple that has been rebuilt in Jerusalem after the exile but he is obviously somewhat disappointed with it. The post-exilic restoration has achieved only moderate success. He believes Jerusalem is still an afflicted Holy City awaiting mercy[104] and he considers those within it to still be "captives" and "distressed".[105] The exile has not truly ended. A return to Jerusalem in its present condition is not desirable. The narrator envisages a new glorious Temple, much greater than the original one, that will mark the eschatological age. At that time,

> the nations in the whole world will all be converted and worship God in truth....Israelites... will be gathered together; they will go to Jerusalem and live in safety forever in the land of Abraham and it will be given over to them.[106]

The author of *Tobit* thus prophesies and longs for a glorious journey of return to Jerusalem. Significantly, he does not simply envisage a journey of return to what was before the exile. It is not a longing for the good old days, for everything to be as it was. Wiser for the exile experience, the author longs for a restored Temple and city that will greatly surpass the original, pre-exilic ones and which will embrace all of the peoples of the world.

No such prophetic vision of a journey of return to Jerusalem can be found in *Esther*. As previously mentioned, the narrator's concern is for the exiles to stay where they are. To understand the narrator's position we need to consider some of the tensions that existed between Jews in Palestine and Jews in the Diaspora during the fourth century BCE.

As we can see from the books of *Chronicles*, the returned exiles in Palestine maintained that they best represented the elect community of God. God was accessible through prayer and, especially, through Temple cult. Those who chose to remain in "exile" in the Diaspora put themselves outside the chosen community.[107]

The narrator of *Esther* strongly rejects such a notion. He stresses that God is continuing to act on behalf of Diaspora Judaism. Furthermore, by stressing Mordecai's descent from the original exiles he is affirming the continuity between pre-exilic and Diaspora communities. He even goes so far as to assert the superiority of the Jewish community in Persia over the one in Palestine. He repeatedly emphasises that Esther's actions save all of the Jews in the empire, by inference those in Palestine as well.[108] He portrays a proud, self-contained and independent Jewish community in Susa that has no interest in looking to Judah for advice, much less approval. He affirms that the community is not in exile from God and creates a vision of the land of exile becoming the promised land. Twice he speaks of conversions *en masse* of gentiles to Judaism. S. D. Goitein, in fact, suggests that the frequent banqueting in *Esther* is an oblique suggestion that the Diaspora has become the land of milk and honey.[109] This may be extreme but it does suggest the direction of the narrator's thinking.

6

A biblical spirituality of exile

Having described and examined the experience of exile in the stories of *Tobit* and *Esther*, we can now ask: what is the spirituality that emerges in these stories?

Accepting the definition of spirituality as the human person's capacity for self-transcending integration in relation to the Ultimate, we must say that the books of *Esther* and *Tobit* provide us with wonderful examples of spiritual persons. Esther transcended herself by risking her life and comfortable station as Queen for the well being of the Jewish people. Tobit also risked his life for his fellow Jews by removing their bodies and burying them in defiance of the King. He was forced to flee and had his property confiscated.[110] Tobias and Sarah also placed obedience to the Torah and to their parents above their personal safety. Tobias risked his life by undertaking a dangerous journey in obedience to his father's request and he further risked his life by marrying Sarah in accordance with the Law even though her previous seven husbands had been killed by the demon, Asmodeus, on their wedding night. Likewise Sarah, in obedience to her parents, risked further humiliation by marrying Tobias. All of these people transcended their own sense of personal well being for the good of others. Put another way, by emptying themselves they enriched their communities and were self-fulfilled.[111]

Significantly, especially in *Esther*, the Ultimate to which they transcend themselves is not God but the Jewish people. The ultimate good is the continued existence of the Jews in exile. It is important to appreciate, however, that for the Semitic mind God can only be conceived of in relationship. A philosophical understanding of God-in-God's-Self was totally foreign to them. God for them is the God of Abraham, Isaac and Jacob, the God of the Covenant. They can only know God in relationship with God's people. In the preservation of the people lies the preservation of the relationship with God. Thus we have a human and a religious spirituality intimately entwined, indeed one. Self-transcendence in relation to the Jewish people is self-transcendence in relation to God. Exile is thus both a God issue and a community issue in one.

It is important to note that these acts of self-transcendence are intimately related to the experience of exile. They arose because of exile, not despite it. Exile provided the seed bed which, in fact, facilitated a deeper spirituality than that which previously existed. This is especially noticeable in *Tobit*. It is precisely the misfortunes of Tobit that force him to send his son on a journey to Rages to collect the money. As it turns out, the rewards of the trip far exceed its original objective. Not only is the money collected but, more importantly, Tobias obtains the remedy for his father's blindness, he meets and marries Sarah reuniting families separated by exile and ensuring the continuance of the Jewish race, and he removes the shame and grief of Sarah and her parents. None of these wonderful things would have happened if misfortune had not engulfed Tobit. The narrator is stressing that exile, though terrible, can also be a source of wonderful fruit.

The same point is made in the narrator's choice of the genre of romantic quest to describe the journey of Tobias.[112] In this genre the quester always encounters a foe who threatens the quester's life. Once conquered the foe becomes an ally, often a source of life and healing. In Tobias' case the foe is a sea monster, a big fish that leaps out of the water and attacks him.[113] Tobias battles with the fish and kills it. He then extracts from the fish the gall, heart and liver which will be used in the healing of Tobit and Sarah. The fish, once a foe, thus becomes the agent of healing. The application to exile is clear: though initially a foe, the exile can be a means of purification, of healing for the Jewish people, a time to remove their blindness. It is not beyond this narrator's imagination to give the exile experience some of the characteristics of a quest. As already noted, the narrator is not simply interested in a restoration of what was before but in the establishment of a more glorious Jerusalem. Exile offers such transcending possibilities.

There are other reasons why exile offers such possibilities for self-transcendence. Exile is a time of *marginality* in which one cannot look to external structures – government, monarchy, Temple – for support. To survive one must turn to previously untapped inner, personal resources. As Esther discovered, our inner resources are great and we can accomplish much more than we previously thought possible. We amaze ourselves; we transcend the personal limits that once defined us.

Another great benefit of exile is that it is a time of *honesty*. In the face of catastrophe we cannot simply accept the old facile explanations. Answers must be found if we are to remain within our religious and cultural tradition. A *translation*, a reformulation of religious belief, must happen in the light of the new situation. Survival demands a transcending of older religious positions. Despite all its pain, exile is a time of opportunity for reconsidering faith and the issues of life.

We must note also the importance of *story* for this reformulation of belief and Jewish identity in the post-exilic period. In the absence of laws addressing the peculiarities of Jewish life in the Diaspora, "Jews in exile used stories to shape behaviour and attitudes and to come to grips with certain questions of great urgency."[114] The stories of *Tobit* and *Esther* are two fine examples of Diaspora stories. At the level of families, communal story telling also played an important role in helping to ensure Jewish survival in exile.

Our study of exile in the books of *Tobit* and *Esther* has also revealed a *variety* of responses to exile. If we were to study other biblical works of the exilic and post-exilic period, we would find different responses again. This is perfectly valid. The Jewish people appreciated that the pain of exile and the crisis it engendered were "too deep to admit of only one response."[115] Accordingly, exile will also produce a variety of expressions of spirituality, all of which are potentially valid.

One expression, found in *Tobit*, looks to a return of exiles to Jerusalem and emphasises the observance of Torah and Jewish practices of piety. The importance of prayer in all its forms – lament, petition, thanksgiving, praise and blessing – is highlighted.

Another spirituality of exile, typified in *Esther*, recognises that the activity of God is inextricably entwined with the activity of humans. This spirituality calls for the creative use of all of one's personal resources – initiative, courage, cunning, beauty, intelligence. In this spirituality, which does not envisage a physical return as being part of the solution to exile, adaptability is an important quality, as is the ability to work productively in a foreign environment.

Remembering and *anticipating* are also important aspects of an exile spirituality. Remembering plays an important role in *Tobit*. The turnaround in fortunes began on the day Tobit remembered the money he had left in trust with Gabael at Rages in Media.[116] On his wedding night Tobias "remembered the words of Raphael, and took the fish's liver and heart out of the bag where he had put them and put them on the embers of the incense."[117] In exile it is important to remember God's saving deeds in past events: remembering makes the event, and its saving power, present.

Exile is also a time of anticipation. Both stories have an eschatological character. They proclaim the eventual victory of God's people. Hope is a very important quality in exile. As Klein has noted, "exile is a time for hope, not triumphalism."[118] *Patience* is needed.

Remembering God's saving deeds in the past, aware of God's activity in the present and firm in the hope of ultimate victory means that, despite its difficulties, exile is a time of *celebration*. A celebratory aspect will always be a part of exile spirituality. Banqueting and feasting play important roles in both *Tobit* and *Esther*. In faith the Jews can celebrate their anticipated victory over their enemies during the feast of Purim. This carnival-like celebration with its costumes and disguises and joyous character was originally a Babylonian or Persian ritual which Jews in the Diaspora adopted and transformed into a Jewish feast. During Purim "the Talmud permits the free consumption of wine to the point where the distinction between 'Blessed be Mordecai' and 'Cursed be Haman' becomes blurred."[119] The mere fact of survival, coping with the challenges of one's moment in history, is indeed reason to celebrate. But Purim suggests more. Exile is not only a time for surviving but for living as fully as one can.

Tobit reminds us that at the family level also, there are many reasons for exiles to celebrate: weddings, the re-unification of families, and experiences of healing are all occasions to break into celebration. In keeping with the injunction of *Deuteronomy* to "rejoice before the Lord your God,"[121] celebration in *Tobit* is also an expression of covenantal joy.

In both stories, banquets have empowering/disempowering motifs. There is a healing power in the celebration. In *Esther* the second banquet of King Ahasuerus provoked the deposition of Queen Vashti and the emergence of Esther. Esther's second banquet led to the demise of Haman and the rise of Mordecai. In *Tobit* the fourteen day wedding feast for Tobias and Sarah signifies both the disempowering of the demon, Asmodeus, and the empowering of Tobias and Sarah to take their rightful place in Israel as parents. To feast is to savour the sweet taste of victory, and to make the victory more real.

Finally an element of *humour* should not be absent from exile spirituality. The use of humour is an important device for the narrator of *Esther*. Robert Alter speaks of the "comic art" of *Esther*, noting that the story is "richly embellished with satiric invention."[122] To miss the satire is to miss much of the humour and also much of the story's message. *Esther* has often been condemned for its very negative presentation of women. Such condemnations completely miss the satire. The narrator is, in fact, parodying Persian attitudes towards women. Through his portrayal of Esther as a courtly sage he is, in fact, offering a positive appreciation of women for his time. The author also makes skilful and humorous use of irony. A striking example is Haman who throughout the story seeks to be elevated to ever greater heights in the kingdom. In the end Haman is truly elevated higher than anyone else, fifty cubits high on the gallows he had prepared for Mordecai! Bruce Jones has noted that we still "know too little about the nature of humour in the ancient world."[123] But clearly, for the author of *Esther*, it is much easier to bear the pain of subjugation if you can mock the follies and excesses of your oppressors.

The story of *Tobit* is more human than humorous, with many heartwarming incidents, but there is plenty to smile about: Tobit's being blinded by bird droppings of all things, the dog who accompanies Tobias and Raphael on their journey, and Sarah's father, Raguel, digging a grave for Tobias in the middle of the night and then filling it in, and so on. The narrator of *Tobit* also appreciates that humour can help to make exile more bearable. It has a rightful place in exile spirituality.

This completes our study of the ancient biblical experience of exile and the spirituality which derives from it, a study which provides an important referent for the primary task of this work – an exploration of Australian spirituality through a study of two modern Australian novels, *Cloudstreet* and *Woman of the Inner Sea*. To this task we must now turn.

PART TWO

A MODERN EXPERIENCE OF EXILE: LIVING IN AUSTRALIA

7

Exiled to Australia

On 13 May, 1787, a fleet of eleven ships left Portsmouth, England, bound for a non-existent colony on the unexplored Australian continent. Among the 1,030 people on board were 736 convicts (548 male and 188 female) being taken into exile.

Social inequities in Georgian England had produced a vast underclass and a swelling wave of crime. Transportation – or forced exile – was one of the solutions employed by the Government to cope with vastly overcrowded prisons.

From 1717 to 1775 about forty thousand convicts were transported to plantation owners in the Caribbean and America. When the rebellion of the American colonies stopped the flow of convicts there, the British Government had to find a new place to exile its prisoners. The unexplored Australian continent seemed ideal because of its remoteness from Europe. The thought of projecting this "excrementitious mass" of criminals as far out of sight as possible, was very appealing.[124]

Over the next eighty years the British Crown shipped more than 160,000 men, women and children from England and Ireland in bondage to Australia. As Robert Hughes has noted, "it was the largest forced exile of citizens at the behest of a European Government in pre-modern history."[125] It ended less than 130 years ago, in January, 1868, when the final 279 prisoners were disgorged in Fremantle, near Perth, in the Swan River colony.

In 587 BCE the Babylonians took the leading citizens of Jerusalem into exile and left the lower classes behind. In 1787 the British Government shipped its lowest class into exile that the leading citizens might feel more comfortable at home. The Babylonian exiles took a religious consciousness with them and wrestled with the implications of exile for their relationship with God. The Australian penal colony was largely devoid of religious inspiration. The Governor and officers in charge were products of the Enlightenment, men of cool reason who had little time for the consolations of religion.[126]

The Jewish exiles were transported a mere eight hundred miles into another part of what was still the known world. The first convicts who were exiled to Australia were sent to a continent whose outline had never been traced and whose interior had never been explored by Europeans. Great and fearful stories circulated in England about what people might encounter on this southern continent – demons, beasts, even hell itself.[127] In an era when most people rarely travelled more than ten miles from their place of birth, these convicts were taken on a fourteen thousand mile journey to a place they knew nothing about. It felt like they were being sent to another planet, an exiled world.[128] When they set anchor at Sydney Cove on 26 January, 1788, all this new place had in common with England was that there was sky above and earth below.

For the convicts, the reluctant soldiers sent to control them, and the officers in charge of the colony, the first days in Australia were extremely harsh. As W. T. Tyler has noted, "starvation, savagery and death" characterised the new colony.[129] The convicts did, however, reveal "an astonishing will to survive."[130] Gradually they managed to achieve a measure of self-sufficiency in their inhospitable new place of residence.

In time, the colony began to develop materially and many of the convicts, like their Babylonian counterparts, chose to remain in the land of their exile once they had served their sentences. Despite the injustices and the general harshness of life in the new colony, it did offer a fresh start to many thousands of poor people who would have been crushed in spirit and destined for a life of crime and imprisonment in England.[131] In the Australian colonies they had the chance to own some land, learn a trade and make a life for themselves. Some became quite prosperous within a few years of obtaining their freedom.

Since the Australian exiles were free to return home once their sentences had expired, and since the population of the Australian colonies was also bolstered in time by the arrival of free settlers, the question can be asked of them that was asked of Jews living in the Diaspora after 539 BCE: can they and their descendants rightly be called exiles?

While today many white Australians would not consider themselves to be exiles, the Australian novel, *Cloudstreet*, suggests that they remain strangers and aliens. After two hundred years they still do not belong to the land.

Cloudstreet tells the story of two battling Australian families, the Pickles and the Lambs, who have been exiled by circumstances from their rural homes in Western Australia and forced to move to Perth where they share a house on Cloud Street. Early in the story it becomes apparent that Cloudstreet,[132] as the house comes to be called, represents the Australian continent. The Pickles' family feel:

the big emptiness of the house around them, almost
paralysing them with spaces and surfaces that yield
nothing to them. It's just them in this vast indoors.[133]

These images are suggestive of the Australian
continent with its vast interior, its barren and seemingly
ungiving character. It becomes clear at this early stage
that while the Pickles own Cloudstreet:

this great continent of a house doesn't belong to them.
They're lost.[134]

Later, their tenants, the Lamb family, verbalise the
same experience. Lester Lamb and his wife, Oriel,
wonder why the house moans. Lester asks:

You think maybe we don't belong here, like we're out
of our depths, out of our country?[135]

Lester has articulated a crucial question underlying
the text of *Cloudstreet*: is it possible for non-Aboriginal
Australians to belong to this land? The inference is that
they do not yet belong, that they remain aliens and
exiles

Cloudstreet is set in a twenty year period from 1943 to
1963, a time when the majority of white Australians
were of Anglo or Celtic origin. The great wave of
refugees who fled to Australia from Europe in the years
following the Second World War do not make a significant impact on the wider community until after the
time span of *Cloudstreet*. However, in the second novel
under study, *Woman of the Inner Sea*, which is set in the
1990s, this new wave of immigrants has made its
presence felt changing the character of Sydney, bringing
new ways of doing business, new cuisines, and
changing some of the unwritten laws of life in Sydney.

Despite these exterior changes, however, the narrator
of *Woman of the Inner Sea* believes that the Sydney of the

1990s bears striking similarities to the Sydney of the old convict days. As Tyler writes:

> In Keneally's modern Sydney, the ancestry of the original jailbirds has mixed with other migrants, and energy and commerce have infused the city with a new barbarism. Acquisitiveness, greed and commercial exploitation now drive the future and keep the present generation in unredeemed if unconscious bondage.[135]

Explaining his attitude to history in writing fiction, the author of *Woman of the Inner Sea*, Thomas Keneally, has noted that he looks "to find evidence in earlier events for the kind of society we have now."[136] This statement provides an important key for understanding *Woman of the Inner Sea*. Looking at the behaviour of many of Sydney's present residents, the narrator of this story sees the savagery, greed and moral bankruptcy that characterised the original convict settlement. The narrator levels this charge at both the new and older inhabitants of the city, denouncing the illegal activities of both the not-so-Reverend Frank, the Celtic uncle of the story's hero, Kate Gaffney-Kozinsky, and her Polish-Australian husband, Paul. Both end the story in prison confirming their convict status.

This evil, alienating environment claims its victims. The hero, Kate Gaffney-Kozinsky, suffers the most terrible loss a mother can experience. Her two children, whom she treasured more than anything, are burned to death in a deliberately set house fire. Unaware of what caused the fire, Kate assumes the burden of responsibility and guilt. The tragedy is so great that Kate cannot talk or even think about it. She can survive only by putting distance between herself and her feelings. She also has no choice but to flee the city and the people associated with the unspeakable event. She takes a train inland seeking anonymity and escape from her self, the person she believes is responsible for the death of her children.

Kate's flight from Sydney is not the only exile story in *Woman of the Inner Sea*. Many of the inhabitants of Sydney are in bondage to evil and unable to form a just community. They too are in exile, though unaware of the fact. Kate's journey to the interior is symbolic of the inner journey they all must take if they are to be set free.

We will study in detail now the stories of *Cloudstreet* and *Woman of the Inner Sea*. To facilitate dialogue with the biblical texts we will ask of them the same questions that we asked of the books of *Tobit* and *Esther* noting, at each step, the different nuances of the questions underlying these stories.

8

Where is God in all this?

As with the biblical stories we have looked at, the God question looms large in *Cloudstreet*. One of the families, the Lambs, are introduced by the narrator as "God-fearing people".[137] As members of the Church of Christ, they belong to the evangelical Christian tradition with its emphasis on the Bible as the only pure source of revelation.

Like Tobit and Job, the Lambs are virtuous, conscientious and hard working but, as with their biblical counterparts, God fails to produce the good in their lives. Their farm collapses and then the only miracle that ever happened to them – the return to life of one of their sons, Fish, after drowning – proves to be no miracle at all. Humiliated, the Lambs are forced to leave the town in which they live, they are forced into exile:

> You can't stay in a town when everything blows up in your face – especially the only miracle that ever happened to you.[138]

Their deepest pain, however, is their sense of alienation, of exile, from God:

> There they were.
> The Lambs of God.
> Except no one believes any more: the
> disappointment has been too great.[140]

The Lambs decide they no longer believe in a good God. They will spend the rest of the story desperately trying to maintain that position. Ironically, as the Lambs will discover, the God question underlying *Cloudstreet* is not: is it possible to believe? Rather, is it possible *not* to believe?

In *Tobit* God sent an angel, Raphael, to bring healing and guidance to the Jewish families in exile. Something similar happens in *Cloudstreet*. As Christina Thompson notes:

> There is an Aboriginal character in *Cloudstreet* who appears spontaneously at critical moments, delivers his message and goes again by means which are entirely unclear. He is a kind of angel – in a sense a guardian, but then again not quite. His message has to do with the business of belonging to people, to families, to places. His presence exerts an almost physical pressure on the families in *Cloudstreet* when they threaten to fly apart.[141]

When guilt forces one of the Lamb children, Quick, to flee from Cloudstreet, he frequently encounters the black man. As with Tobias, Quick has an angel with him on his journey though he fails to recognise the fact. Throughout the story the Aboriginal frequently speaks to Quick, always urging him to go back to Cloudstreet, but for the most part Quick refuses to listen. Indeed, at times he refuses to believe that the Aboriginal is even there. Unlike Tobias, who obeys the every directive of Raphael, Quick does not act on anything the Aboriginal says until near the end of the story. When a serial killer is on the loose and everyone is fearful, the black man appears to Quick again:

> You've got a home to go to, Quick. Go there.
> Quick regarded the man. He was naked enough to arrest
> Go there.
> Orrigght, said P.C. Quick, already on his way.[142]

Finally, Quick listens, and he takes himself and his wife, Rose, back to Cloudstreet. It has been hard for Quick to listen to the Aboriginal. He was, after all, "a black man."[143] Quick's attitude mirrors that of many white Australians who look down on Aboriginals as ignorant, backward people. Yet, the story of *Cloudstreet* only comes to its happy conclusion when people start to listen to the black man, first Quick and then Sam Pickles, the legal owner of Cloudstreet who, after twenty years, is considering selling the house. The Aboriginal confronts Sam with a direct message: "You shouldn't break a place. Places are strong, important."[144] His words have an effect on Sam. Later, Sam's wife, Dolly, confirms the Aboriginal's advice. Surprising even herself, she urges Sam not to sell the house. Sam acts on the Aboriginal's advice and decides not to sell.

In portraying the Aboriginal as a guardian and speaker of wisdom the narrator is stressing that non-Aboriginal Australians must listen to the wisdom of the Aboriginal people in order to believe and belong in Australia. The Aboriginal people have inhabited the Australian continent for at least forty thousand years, non-Aboriginals for a mere two hundred years. The Aboriginals have learned to belong to the land and have experienced its sacredness. If non-Aboriginal Australians are to cease to be exiles, they must learn from the Aboriginals to belong to the land.

When we meet the Lamb family in *Cloudstreet* they are alienated not only from God, but also from the land. Indeed, the land seems to shut down when they are around. The Lambs enter a scene and suddenly:

> all around, the bush has gone the colour of a cold roast. Bird's scuffle out of sight. There's no wind.[145]

Later, when Quick observes the hardness of his relatives, Earl and May, he concludes that "the land has done this to them....this could have been us."[146] Shortly after, however, Quick, who is working with Earl and May:

dreams he is asleep, and in that sleep he is dreaming a
dream: there they all are, down by the river laughing
and chiacking about, all of them whole and true, with
their own faces in a silver rain of light fused with birds
and animals. Lester, Oriel, Hat, Elaine, Lon, Red, Fish,
himself and people he doesn't know: women with
babies, old people, men with their sleeves pinned,
barefoot children, all moving behind a single file of
other people the colour of burnt wood. Down at the
river where the fish are leaping and the sea has turned
back on itself and the trees shake with music.[147]

This is a dream of enlightenment. Quick sees a human
race made up of countless people, including his family,
Aboriginals and people he doesn't know belonging and
being together. Not only is there a communion among
people but a connectedness with nature as well. The
land is not an enemy but alive with spirit. Recognising
the sacred in nature will be an essential component in
the healing of the Lambs' sense of alienation from God.

Quick's dream occurs at the midpoint of the story.
Gradually the characters will respond to the sacredness
of the land throughout the rest of the story. Most
especially, they will be touched by the sacred character
of water, of the river. In this story the river is alive with
spirit. For the characters of *Cloudstreet* the river is the
sacred place, the place of revelation, the place of the
miraculous, the place of regeneration. When Quick
returns to Cloudstreet after running away, he has four
deep candid conversations with the people who are
dear to him – his mother, Oriel, his father, Lester, his
brother, Fish, and his future wife, Rose – and they all
take place on the river. It is on the river that Rose and
Quick decide to get married, a union so important for
healing the divisions of the characters in this story. The
river, the beautiful, the beautiful river that meanders

through Perth is a spirit-filled presence for the people of Cloudstreet, indeed for all the inhabitants of that city. If only they can see it.

Gradually Quick comes to appreciate the spirit-filled significance of the river:

> He was comfortable out there on the water, alone with the city lights and the quiet pressure of the outgoing tide. The river was a broad, muttering, living thing always suggesting things that kept his mind busy. Every important thing that happened to him, it seemed, had to do with a river. It was insistent, quietly forceful like the force of one's own blood. Sometimes he thought of it as the land's blood: it roiled with life and living.[148]

While greatly respecting the spiritual wisdom of the Aboriginal people, the narrator of *Cloudstreet* does not denigrate the Judeo-Christian religious tradition. Rather, he hints at connections between the two traditions. In *Cloudstreet* the Aboriginal performs many of the same actions that Christ performs in the Gospels. The Aboriginal walks on water,[149] waits at the seashore for Quick,[150] offers Quick a meal of bread and wine which brings comfort[151] and later appears to Quick wearing only a towel and a pair of thongs[152] reminiscent of the Last Supper when Christ removed his outer garment and, clad only in a towel, gave his disciples an example of service.[153] The Aboriginal's message on the importance of family is consistent with the Gospel emphasis on the importance of community – "may they all be one".[154] The story of *Cloudstreet* is replete with biblical allusions.

Towards the end of the story Lester and Oriel Lamb move back towards their Christian tradition. The *King James Bible* is with Oriel in the tent. She opens it and takes consolation in knowing that the names of the members of her family are recorded in it.[155] Her husband, Lester, starts visiting a cathedral on Sunday mornings. As he looks at the gorgeous vaulted ceilings and the ceremonies he feels "the pleasantest kind of melancholy" and "homesickness".[156]

For the narrator of *Cloudstreet* the problem is not a concealed God, as it was for the characters of *Tobit* and *Esther*. As the Aboriginal people have discovered, all of creation is spirit-filled. What people must do is look, see, feel, dream and believe what they experience. The problem is not the absence of God but not knowing where and how to look for the Sacred. This is something the Aboriginal people can teach white Australians, many of whom, like the Lambs, are finding that the God images of their European heritage fail to speak adequately to their present experience.

For the narrator of *Cloudstreet* the coastal city of Perth is a sacred place. The Swan river which flows through Perth is spirit-filled. The narrator is adamant that one does not have to go to the interior of the continent to find the Sacred. Indeed, for the characters to go inland beyond rivers, beyond rain and pleasure, is for them to go "out to where they are homeless, where they have never belonged".[157]

The narrator of *Woman of the Inner Sea* presents a very different viewpoint. For him the coastal city of Sydney is a moral wasteland, spiritually bankrupt. Despite the presence of some good people, one must leave the city and journey inland to find honesty, innocence, safety and true community values:

> This Celtic city – named Sydney by accidents of history and displaced to the Southwest Pacific – really worshipped scoundrel gods and tart goddesses

and only gave token nods to the Other, the Dressed-up One.[158]

Kate's journey to the interior mirrors the inward journey of the spiritual quest in *Woman of the Inner Sea*. As Kate was led away, groaning and wailing, from the charred remains of the fire in which her children were killed, a shocking awareness came over her: "Nothing at all, she found to her dread, lay at the base of that wail."[159] It seemed that everything had been taken away from her. Although she was unaware of it at the time, her survival will depend on her finding something at the base of that wail, some source of life deep within herself. As with Queen Esther, she will survive the evil activities of men only by finding within herself the personal resources she needs to meet the challenge of survival and to bring just retribution to the murderers of her children.

Early indications are that Kate's journey to her spiritual core will be very slow. The reader experiences frustration at the narrator's refusal to describe the core event of the story, the death of her children. Aware of the reader's impatience, the narrator says at one stage, "We're getting to the core, the frightful trigger."[160] But he still takes another 150 pages to do so. Kate will also take a long time to reach her spiritual core, just as it took time for Queen Esther to mature into the wise sage able to save her people.

The reader is also discouraged by Kate's decision to exit the train before it has completed its journey to the interior. At that stage she was not able to go all the way to her own inner core. She alights at Myambagh, a town that has a familiar feel to her. Once settled in the town, she is still focusing on the surface of things. She wants to change her exterior appearance by excessive eating.

She is trying to change her self, the self that carelessly let her children die, but she is focusing on her exterior self. She still has no contact with her inner core. In Myambagh Kate takes a room at Murchison's Railway Hotel, owned by Jack Murchison and his wife, Connie. Kate has no interest in getting involved with the people or the life of the town. But she accepts a job serving beer at the hotel. It is a hopeful sign to see this woman who is dammed up pouring liquid refreshment for others.

In Myambah healing begins for Kate. She has time for solitude. She comes to love "her cherished room",[161] her place of solitude. Despite seeking anonymity, she also begins to be touched by the kindness and goodness of the country folk, especially Jack Murchison and Jelly, a gentle, overweight patron of the bar whom Kate takes as "her protector and associate."[162] Jack and Jelly care for Kate without asking questions about her unspeakable past. Gradually, imperceptibly, Kate comes to love Myambagh. As she looks out over the town one morning from the hotel verandah she feels "a pulse in her... a pulse something like love."[163]

In her room one night she reads an encyclopedia entry on kangaroos, which the narrator of *Woman of the Inner Sea* calls "the national totem."[164] Kate experiences "the shadow of rapture" as she reads about the kangaroo. She senses its connection with the earth which it turns with its gentle mouth.[165] In a dream one night a sleek marsupial pride uncoils within her and bounds forward. Reminiscent of Quick's dream of enlightenment in *Cloudstreet*, she experiences a "sweet connection" with the kangaroo which offers her hope of release from the horrible events that weigh her down. Awake, she concludes that the dream was illusory, but "she knew her pleasure was significant."[166]

Shortly after the town is threatened by a massive flood. Kate is quick to join the citizens in building sand levees. It was exhausting work but Kate experiences the ecstasy of communal effort.[167] The skin on her hands tears away in the work, another positive sign. The outer shell is disintegrating. An ambulance officer senses that Kate has sacrificed her hands for Myambagh. He is partially right. Atonement for the sin of being a bad mother is a necessary part of Kate's healing. The flood has offered her the chance to make some atonement.

Kate soon learns that, in life, loss is followed by loss. Having lost her children, she next loses Jelly in a dynamiting accident. Ironically, the town is saved from the flood by the explosion which kills him, but the town is lost to her. The circumstances surrounding the accident force her to flee Myambagh and go deeper into the interior with Gus Schulberger, a battling farmer, and two animals, Chiffley, a kangaroo, and Menzies, an emu, refugees like her from the bestiality of humans.

Circumstances are forcing Kate deeper into the interior, a journey she was not able to make when she first fled Sydney. On this journey the kangaroo, Chiffley, has a deep impact on her. She notices that he had entered a new phase of meditation, something that is also happening to her on this journey. For a long time she had not been able to think about her marriage, her children, or the unspeakable tragedy. Now, memories and thoughts return and she lets them happen. This new found ability to think about the past is both a sign that healing is happening and an agent in further healing. When she reaches the isolated homestead owned by Gus she now has "more time for recollection than she had been permitted in Myambagh, or had permitted herself."[168]

Gus, her companion on her journey to the deep interior, also touches her deeply with his kindness, his caring and his innocence. He is a very safe person with whom to journey to the deepest interior. While bathing one morning in his house "she washed her genitals and felt the unfamiliar blood in them".[169]

Life is beginning to flow from her interior once again. Gus' home is built on a sea bed that is long dried up. But as Kate gives herself to Gus in sexual union she feels "certain waters breaking and flowing inside her."[170] She has contacted her own living, and life giving, inner sea.

The early explorers of Australia journeyed to the centre of the continent expecting to find a vast inland sea. They discovered to their disappointment that they had arrived two hundred million years too late. Instead of being bathed by water they were blinded by the harshest light.[171] Ironically, in *Woman of the Inner Sea*, Kate Gaffney-Kozinsky journeys to the centre of Australia seeking nothingness and finds instead a life giving inner sea.

We cannot underestimate the role of Chiffley in helping Kate to find her own inner sea. As Susan Fromberg Schaeffer has noted, it is:

> Chiffley, the tame kangaroo, whose ability to leap through the air restores her faith in salvation. Weighed down as she is by guilt, which has slowed and trapped her, she sees Chiffley as something of a god, perhaps her own child, certainly a symbol of freedom.[173]

Shortly after guiding Kate to her own inner sea, Chiffley is put down by Gus in what he believes is a humane act. Kate is devastated. Loss follows loss for her. The loss of Chiffley means that she can bound no further into the interior.[174] Circumstances also take her life with Gus away from her. The time has come to return to Sydney. She goes back dazed, shocked, barely able to breathe. Her re-entry will be extremely difficult. But she will survive. In her time in exile she has discovered within herself a stream of living water that will give her life and further grief. She has a living font within her, inviolate to the touch of evil forces.

It is Kate's uncle, the not-so-Reverend Frank, who correctly discerns that the time has come for Kate to return "home" to Sydney.[175] A challenge for exiles is always to determine what place to call home. The Jewish community of Queen Esther recognised that the land of exile was now their home, while the communities of *Tobit* looked to a return to Jerusalem. Kate faced the difficult recognition that Sydney, the place from which she had fled, the place of so much personal tragedy and evil for her, was also the place where she was called to live. It was home for her. The journey to the interior was necessary for her healing, to help her find her own inner sea. But with her journey's purpose achieved, the time had come for her to return home. It was Uncle Frank who helped her to see this.

In this story the Catholic Church is essentially a fractured Church which has transported centuries old differences from Europe to Australia. It has Irish and Polish forms of expression, and others, which are at loggerheads with each other and within themselves. In himself, Uncle Frank embodies the strengths and the dysfunctionality of the Church. Suspended from priestly duties on account of his illegal gambling activities and his liaison with a widow, Mrs O'Brien, he is also completely self-sacrificing in his love for Kate and is the one person able to help her discern her role in life. Despite all his personal brokenness, he communicates "some mystery of faith" to her.[176]

As with *Cloudstreet*, the narrator of *Woman of the Inner Sea* is not rejecting the Christian tradition but acknowledges the woundedness contained in its present Australian expressions. The narrator is aware also of the need for Australians to have a spiritual connection with the earth, which Kate gains through Chiffley, the Australian totem, if they are to connect with the life giving sea within themselves, a sea that will enable them to cope with life, and find salvation, in the land of their exile.

9

What must people do in exile?

In *Cloudstreet*, Oriel Lamb is the person who does things. A great believer in hard work, she runs her household and the family shop like a sergeant-major.[177] When her drowned son, Fish, is dragged ashore she furiously beats his chest until he begins to breathe again. This refusal on Oriel's part to let nature take its course is tragic for Fish, and for the family. Later, when her other son, Quick, flees Cloudstreet:

> Oriel Lamb, being the sort of woman who resolved to *do* things, decided to make a recovery....She would wipe out the local competition.[178]

Her feverish efforts and those of her family produce success. Her rival, G. M. Clay, is put out of business. Oriel then discovers the tragic consequences of her actions for the Clay family. It seems the harder she works, the more she does, the worse things get.

In her doing, Oriel Lamb typifies many white Australians who have, for two hundred years, sought to do things to the land of their exile, often with tragic consequences for themselves and for the land. They have been ignorant of the Aboriginal wisdom which sees land as a living, spirit-filled reality. One should not do things to a living reality. One should be in relationship with it.

Cloudstreet, which represents the land, is a living, breathing house. It is also a very unhappy house. As Fish Lamb tells his father, Lester:

> The house sad, Lestah.
> What? How dyou know that? [Lester asks]
> It talks.

......
It hurts.[179]

The house is hurting because the actions of people have created divisions within it. Back in time it was owned by a respectable white woman who opened it up to single pregnant Aboriginal girls who were forced to adopt European ways. This estrangement from family and culture was too great for one of the girls who committed suicide. The other girls were evicted and later the old woman died, alone and isolated, in the house. Many years later, when the Pickles take up residence, the spirits of the old woman and the Aboriginal girl remain in the house, torn apart and unreconciled. These past happenings in the house will affect the new residents of Cloudstreet just as people in Australia today, white and black, are affected by the legacy of the past. This legacy will have to be healed for the residents of Cloudstreet to feel at home, and for all Australians to belong in their vast continent.

The house is also unhappy because of the divisions its present occupants have brought to it. To allow for tenants the owner, Sam Pickles, has divided the house down the middle, and has created two yards and built two privies outside. Not only is the house divided, but there are many divisions within and among its inhabitants. The saving actions of Oriel Lamb have divided her son, Fish, in two and also created a deep division between herself and Fish, who doesn't seem to know her anymore. On the Pickles' side of the house, a deep division exists between Rose and her alcoholic mother, Dolly, whom Rose despises for her failure to be a good mother. Both Dolly and Rose risk destroying themselves through illness, Dolly through alcoholism and Rose through anorexia.

To ask of *Cloudstreet*, what must one do in exile, is, therefore, to ask of it precisely the wrong question. It is the actions of people, what they have done to the land and to each other, that create divisions. In the land of their exile, the inhabitants of Cloudstreet are not primarily called to do anything. Rather they are called to see the deep connectedness of all human beings with each other and with the land, and to live in accord with this. The challenge is not to create or produce this connectedness, but to recognise it and not to destroy it by their actions.

Cloudstreet is a story full of connections though for most of the story the characters fail to recognise them. A fishing accident precipitates the tragedy for both families. Fish's actual name is Samson, that is, Sam's son, though he is actually Lester's son. Dolly and her daughter, Rose, share an Aboriginal heritage, though neither see this. When Rose sees the "black and bare" feet of her drunken mother beside the railway tracks she is aware of her mother's squalor but not of her colour.[180] Later, when Rose stands in front of the ice box chipping ice, Dolly sees "the brown sticks of [Rose's] legs".[181] Dolly sees her daughter's anorexic condition but fails to notice the colour that connects mother and daughter.

On the surface the two mothers, Oriel Lamb and Dolly Pickles, are totally different. Yet they too have a deep connection in a childhood grief. Oriel's step mother was young enough to be her sister, while Dolly's mother was in fact her sister. Oriel and Dolly are also unknowingly connected in the demise of the rival shopkeeper, G. M. Clay. While Oriel's actions were destroying his business, his activities with Dolly were destroying his marriage.

Surprisingly, Oriel Lamb and Dolly's daughter, Rose, also have much in common. Both are hardworking determined people who don't believe in surrender. As Elaine Lamb tells Rose, "you remind me so much of mum when she was young."[182] More than the others, Rose can understand why Oriel sleeps outside in a tent: "Yeah, she can see why a woman'd move out there to have some life of her own."[183] Later, when giving birth, Rose sees the deep connection between Oriel and herself, and the Aboriginal girl and the old white woman whose spirits linger in the house. When Rose, who is unaware of her Aboriginal heritage, sees these two strange spiritous women:

> It's like she's looking into the room on herself and Oriel because one is old and the other's a girl, but the girl is black, bruise coloured.[184]

There is a deep connection between Fish, whose wide black eyes peer out from his white body,[185] and the Aboriginal whose white eyes bulge out of his black body.[186] Later, Sam Pickles becomes aware of a connection between the Aboriginal and his father: "Jesus, thought Sam, paint him white and he might be me old man."[187]

When a serial killer's son is drowned, Quick cannot help but think of Fish's drowning. He feels a deep connection with the killer. As he tells Rose:

> We all join up somewhere in the end....It's not us and them anymore. It's us and us and us. It's always us. That's what they never tell you.[188]

Deeply connected to each other, human beings are a community. Community is not something to be created. The task is not to destroy community, not to break it up. As different characters leave Cloudstreet, the house cries out, "wait, wait!"[189] When Sam is thinking of selling the house and breaking up the community, the Aboriginal's message is direct: "You shouldn't break a place. Places are strong, important."[190]

The overriding message of *Cloudstreet*, therefore, is that exiles must see their connection with one another and with the land of their exile. As they see this and live according to it, the land will cease to be a place of exile for them. They will come to belong to the land. Their primary activity is not doing, but seeing, responding and being in relationship with the land and with one another.

It will take time for this awareness to become explicit. Cloudstreet cannot be sold for twenty years, and only at the end of that time do the inhabitants start to feel at home. Likewise it will take time for the inhabitants of Australia to feel at home in their continent. Wait, wait, is the message the land is giving to the inhabitants of Australia. Despite the pain it feels from the past and present activities of its inhabitants, the land is not urging them to leave. Incredibly, the land loves those poor, lost souls who are struggling to find their place within it.

While *Cloudstreet* triumphs being over doing, it is not totally negative on human activity. The Aboriginal works hard to keep the inhabitants of Cloudstreet together. Oriel's hard work also bears some good fruit. When the Lambs open a shop in the house on Cloud Street, the shop becomes a centre of community, a place where people meet: "After a time the shop *was* Cloud Street, and people said it, Cloudstreet, in one word."[191] The two words become one through the activities of Oriel and her family. Later, Sam and Dolly Pickles reluctantly admit that they have survived in the house for so long thanks to the activity of their tenants, the Lamb family. As Dolly says:

What's kept us alive is that friggin woman. A dead
man and an ugly woman. Vanilla ice-cream, pasties
and mullet.[192]

People do have to work to survive in the land of their
exile. But they must work with, and not against, their
environment. *Cloudstreet* is a community novel in which
no single character can be called the hero. The role of the
Aboriginal is important, but so is that of Fish, Rose,
Oriel, Quick or the other characters in their own way.
The narrator's conviction is that community is realised
when everyone pitches in and plays their part.

A final activity that is very important is *Cloudstreet* is
talking. Through talking one discovers, or becomes
aware of, connections. As the book's dust jacket says,
the story is noticeable for its "fiery working class collo-
quialisms", or its "Australian tongues", as one reviewer
describes it.[193] Despite many differences the characters,
including the Aboriginal, speak the same idiom. For
much of the story, however, the characters remain
inarticulate.[194] A breakthrough happens when Rose gets
a job on the switchboard at a department store. As she
talks to callers on the switchboard, connecting them to
the people with whom they need to speak, "Rose
Pickles discovered that she could really talk".[195]
Something is released within her and within a short
time the anorexic Rose "puts on a bit of flesh. She eats.
The world lookalienatedent."[196]

Much later, her mother, Dolly, pleads with Rose: "I
want to talk, just to talk."[197] Rose reluctantly agrees and
hears for the first time that Dolly is a child of incest.
Hearing this, "Rose felt things falling within her, a
terrible shifting of weights".[198]

Rose and her mother begin to talk more regularly.

Rose was glad of those talks with her mother. She found soft parts still left in herself, soft parts in Dolly as well, and in a way she figured it saved her from herself. It was love really, finding some love left. It was like tonic.[199]

Then Rose and her husband, Quick, begin to talk to each other like never before. "They talked like teenagers, catching up, making up time, finding words for how they felt."[200] Through words the characters name the feelings they have and find within themselves the love that has been present all along. They discover the deep connections that exist among them.

In her mother's grief, Rose sees "the huge wordless grief of babies",[201] something she has also seen in Fish Lamb, thus highlighting another connection, this time between Fish and Dolly. This phrase also connects this story with *Woman of the Inner Sea* where we again encounter the huge wordless grief of babies and of their mother and of innocent beasts. In this story speech is a vital activity Kate must perform in exile. In the Preface to the original edition of this book,[202] the author notes that Kate has suffered "an unspeakable tragedy". To heal her self-alienation Kate must tell the story of what happened to her children. She has to acknowledge to another the pain and guilt she feels for being away from her children at the time of the fire. Only by telling the story can she reclaim her children[203] and grieve over their death.

In *Woman of the Inner Sea*, the narrator cannot tell Kate's story. It is Kate's responsibility. As with the story of *Esther* human responsibility cannot be avoided. Great patience is required from the reader. It is not until near the end of the novel that Kate is able to tell what happened on the tragic night. The reader must allow her that time.

Much will happen to Kate in exile before she is able to speak the unspeakable. Much of it will be passive. As with *Cloudstreet*, it will not be a case of her doing things but of a healing environment doing things to her. In Myambagh she will be loved and cared for by Jelly and Jack Murchison. She will be forced by circumstances to flee further into the interior where once again she will find loving companions in Gus and Chiffley.

A most important exile activity for Kate will simply be to find time for solitude. Her journey into exile is a journey away from a community that was suffocating and poisoning her, a community that destroyed her children. Unlike *Cloudstreet*, with its strong emphasis on community, *Woman of the Inner Sea* triumphs the importance of solitude, of stepping aside from community, for salvation.

Of course, community also plays a positive role in *Woman of the Inner Sea*. Kate's involvement in the community in Myambagh is healing for her and she has good companions on every step of her journey.

Likewise, *Cloudstreet* attributes value to solitude for a time. It is while Quick is in the country, away from Cloudstreet, that he comes to see the connectedness of all creation. He also came to see that he was homesick as a dog.[204] Despite the pain and suffering that went with belonging to Cloudstreet, Quick realises that there is something good there that he is missing terribly. He ends his solitude and returns to the community.

Quick's Mother, Oriel, is completely committed to her family. She could never leave them, but she too felt the need for solitude, "to have a life of her own", as Rose describes it.[205] Oriel's solution is to live in a tent outside the house at night. Perhaps more than any other character in either story she balances the dual needs of belonging to community and having solitude. But with the passing of years the canvas walls of her tent become thinner and her privacy disappears. Eventually she folds up the tent and moves back into the house. In *Cloudstreet*, ultimately, community has a greater value than solitude. The reverse is the case in *Woman of the Inner Sea*. Though Kate returns to Sydney she does not fully re-enter her former community. In the opening chapter of the book, which tells the end of the story, she is alone on a city street, weeping and separate from the people around her. She will survive in Sydney, not primarily because of community support, but because of the resources she has discovered within herself.

In solitude Kate comes to understand the importance of speech. She must speak for herself and for her children, the innocents who cannot speak. It is the silent kangaroo, Chiffley, who imposes the duty of speech on Kate. She hears an Aboriginal story of how the animals decided to give the gift and duty of language to humans. The kangaroo was selected by the other animals to persuade humans to take on the business of talking. Hearing this story, Kate:

> knows now in an instant what Chiffley's placid intensity meant. It was a kind of persuasion. It was the urging of language upon her. It meant that she cannot merely bellow in distress. Through Chiffley's bestial cunning, she is faced now with the duty of defining her misfortune in words. She is stuck with language and with the aweful business, the fussiness of definition. The cruelty of this stings and distracts her. At once she begins weeping.[206]

In this story Chiffley is a "totem creature".[207] He is something of a god and his silent presence is reminiscent of the concealed God in *Esther*. Like God in *Esther*, Chiffley demands that Kate must act and her activity is speech. In this story also, human responsibility and divine initiative are intertwined. For Kate Gaffney-Kozinsky the most important thing she must do in exile is tell, and own, her story. Once she does this, the peripatetic principle comes to the fore in this story also, and fortunes begin to reverse.

By truthfully telling her story Kate offers an example to the many citizens of Sydney who remain in bondage to evil. As Fromberg Schaeffer has pointed out, the narrator of this story is highly critical of modern urban life as "a wasteland in which people no longer speak the truth".[208] Healing and freedom will come for these exiles when they learn to speak the truth and act with justice.

10

How should non-Aboriginal Australians relate to the Aboriginal people?

An important question underlying the books of *Tobit* and *Esther* is: how should Jews in exile relate to the gentile State? In both stories the Jews found themselves in a position of inferiority and subordination to their gentile overlords. They were the weaker group trying to survive under foreign control.

This was not the experience of the white Australian exiles who quickly came to dominate the indigenous peoples. While not belonging to the land themselves, these exiles from Europe managed to exile many of the Aboriginal people from their own land, both geographically and spiritually. In *Cloudstreet*, the alcoholism and the meaningless, directionless life of Dolly Pickles mirrors that of many Aboriginal people who have lost touch with their tribal roots and are unable to adjust to the society white Australians have created.

In some areas the dominance of the Aboriginal peoples has been so great that their presence has been largely eliminated. The narrator of *Woman of the Inner Sea* makes no mention of an Aboriginal presence in Sydney. He also portrays Sydney as poisonous and spiritually bankrupt. In the light of the teaching of *Cloudstreet*, one can ask whether there is a connection between this situation and the absence of a large Aboriginal presence.

By contrast *Cloudstreet* has a significant Aboriginal presence. The house in *Cloudstreet* well represents the

Australian continent because it has a past and continuing Aboriginal presence within it. The disturbed spirit of the Aboriginal girl who committed suicide remains in the house, and an Aboriginal presence continues in the current inhabitants through Dolly Pickles and her children.

Dolly is not aware that she is part-Aboriginal, even though her father was "a strong and sunbrown and quiet man"[209] and all her children are dark. Her daughter, Rose, is "a slender, brown girl with straight, black hair,"[210] and her two sons are "rangy, sundark kids."[211] The strongest affirmation of her Aboriginality occurs towards the end of the story, paradoxically in denial. Her husband, Sam, who is white, tells the Lambs that he is not going to sell the house.

> Some Abo told me it wasn't worth the money.
> Actually he said it was bad luck.
> That was me! said Dolly. And I'm no Abo.

Sam replies:

> I dunno. I forget.[212]

In her denigrating remark about 'Abos', Dolly is unwittingly denigrating herself.

The narrator of *Cloudstreet* never explicitly affirms that Dolly and her children are part-Aboriginal. His emphasis is on the connectedness of all people. To distinguish between the Aboriginal and non-Aboriginal inhabitants of Cloudstreet would be to highlight a division and to ignore the deep connectedness of all people regardless of race. Because of this connectedness, *Cloudstreet* testifies that it is possible for Aboriginal and non-Aboriginal Australians to live together in mutually enriching ways.

But the issue of identity is important. Like Dolly, her mother, Rose Pickles is ignorant of her Aboriginal heritage. Though she cannot name it, she experiences the confusion that stems from her alienation from this essential aspect of herself. In a poignant scene early in the story, Dolly is in a hotel room having sex with the pilot of a Catalina aeroplane while Rose is outside in the corridor. Looking at Rose:

> you witness the terrible boiling dark in the schoolgirl's head, the confusion, the feeling, the colour she can't put a name to.[213]

For the narrator of *Cloudstreet*, the domination and dismissal of Aboriginal people by white Australians has been tragic for both groups of people. Non-Aboriginal Australians will remain exiles in this land until they learn to value the wisdom of the indigenous peoples who can show white Australians how to belong to this land and how to recognise its sacredness.

In the book of *Tobit*, we saw the great respect shown by Tobit and his family for Jerusalem. It was a sacred place for them, and also a distant place. Unable to find a similar sacredness in the land of their exile, they longed to return to Jerusalem, they never became fully at home in the land of their exile. Non-Aboriginal Australians will also feel alienated from this continent if they are unable to feel its sacredness and experience a connection with its living spirit. While *Cloudstreet* sees a spiritual connection in water, *Woman of the Inner Sea* highlights a connection with the earth through Australia's totemic animals. The kangaroo and the emu which stand astride Australia's coat of arms remind all Australians of the spiritual connection these creatures offer with the earth, our mother.

11

Is a journey of return
envisaged?

The narrator of *Cloudstreet* does not call for white Australians to leave their land of exile and return to Europe. In an attitude reminiscent of *Esther* he emphasises that it is possible for the land of exile to become their home. Indeed, it is already their home if only they can see it. This is the constant message of the Aboriginal in *Cloudstreet*. Whenever Quick leaves Cloudstreet the black man appears to him and tells him to go home: "You've got a home to go to Quick. Go there."[215]

Returns do, however, play a significant role in this story. One of the most significant returns is that of Rose to her Aboriginal self. An essential aspect of the Aboriginal people is their sense of the family, or tribe, which is in many ways more important than the individual. In her deepest self Rose longs for community. She tries to keep her family together, frequently enduring the humiliation of dragging her drunken mother home from the pub. She cooks a family meal each evening even if no one comes.[216] Whenever, in frustration, she gives up on her family and isolates herself she becomes anorexic and miserable.

Towards the end of the story Rose finally connects with the deepest feelings of her Aboriginal person. She realises that what she has always wanted is to be part of a big family, a tribe. She tells her husband, Quick, that she no longer wants them to live in a separate house away from Cloudstreet. Thinking about Cloudstreet, she tells him:

I like the crowds and the noise....Think of it: I'm in this house with the boy next door and his baby, and I'm not miserable and starving and frightened. I'm right in the middle. It's like a village. I don't know. I have these feelings. I can never explain these feelings.
But you hate family stuff. [says Quick]
Rose laughed. But it's two families. It's a bloody tribe, a new tribe.[217]

Rose is still not aware of her Aboriginal heritage. But she has, in fact, returned to it. She has connected with her deepest feelings. The desire for community is a key aspect of the Aboriginal psyche but it is something dear to the hearts of all of the characters in *Cloudstreet*. Despite the pain, difficulties and frustration involved they all finally decide that they want to stay in, and belong to, this crazy community of Cloudstreet.

Rose's return to her Aboriginal roots is only one of a number of significant returns in *Cloudstreet*. Another very important return of a person to wholeness is that of Fish. As he was drowning in the river Fish experienced himself going through darkness into something warm. His pain ceased and he was hurrying towards "a big friendly womb in the gloom."[218] Suddenly this beautiful experience began to recede and to his horror he found that he was being drawn back. Darkness and pain returned. Brought back to life by his mother's frantic efforts Fish lets out a terrible moan: "Never, never, was there a sadder, more disappointed noise."[219]

It turns out, however, that some of Fish did go forward, beyond space and time. Only a part of Fish returned – a healthy body and some limited powers of speech and cognition. As Bula Maddison has correctly noted,

The separation of Fish from Fish is the most interesting and complex of the novel's divisions, and Fish's yearning for reconciliation in himself is the overarching story line.[220]

The Fish who returns from drowning longs to be reunited with the water. His family are unable to let him go, as they are unable to let go of the guilt they feel about his drowning. Yet Fish has no anger for them, no blame. He brings forgiveness and love. When Quick wakes up from his long sleep after returning to the house, he discovers Fish lying with him.

Quick smells his brother's hair, feels the weight of him against his ribs. It feels like forgiveness, this waking, and Quick is determined not to be embarrassed.[221]

When the families in Cloudstreet find love and community, Fish Lamb is finally free to return to the deeps that beckon him. Once Fish returns to the water his mother, Oriel, is once again able to take up residence in the house. Whatever guilt she carried, and whatever hatred she mistakenly felt from Fish for having forced him back to life, has vanished. She is able to re-enter the home space he has physically departed.

In *Woman of the Inner Sea* Kate eventually returns to Sydney. Her return has little in common with the joyful returns of Quick to Cloudstreet and Tobias to his parents in *Tobit*. Kate is forced to return *home* – "as Uncle Frank himself chose to call it"[222] – stupefied with drugs and scarcely able to breathe. The return is shocking to her system.

In *Woman of the Inner Sea* homecomings are very important but also very difficult. It is significant that "for the author, *Woman of the Inner Sea* is in fact Keneally-come-home."[223] The settings for many of

Thomas Keneally's recent works have been outside Australia: the American Civil War in *Confederates* (1979), Nazi Poland in *Schindler's List* (1982), Eritrea in *Towards Asmara* (1989) and the American South West in *The Place Where Souls Are Born* (1993). *Flying Hero Class* (1991) features Australian Aboriginals but they are trapped in an aeroplane overseas.

One wonders whether Keneally felt the same emotions as Frank Pellegrino, the Australian film maker in *Woman of the Inner Sea*. After a successful Australian debut, Pellegrino has spent many years in Hollywood making successful films, one of which earned him an Oscar. Despite his success overseas, he knew he had to return to Australia. As he told a reporter:

> I've probably been too long absent from my Australian well-springs. I want to go back, gather myself, and make one beautiful Australian film.[224]

He knows he must return even though, as he confided to Kate in an urgent whisper, "he had been kept awake by the terror of coming home."[225]

> This is a bloody tough country to come back to, he would say again and again.[226]

Kate also knows the terror of coming home. Sydney is a "bloody tough country" for her. But like the author, and Frank Pellegrino, she must return home. Her experience in exile has taught her the truthfulness of:

> Uncle Frank's dogma about the *necessary* roles of people, a dogma she has seen fulfilled with Jelly and all the attendant deities of Murchison's Railway Hotel. That not everyone was on earth to save themselves.[227]

People do have roles in this world, vocations or callings. In a story written many years earlier the Jew, Mordecai, had pointed out to his young relative, Queen Esther, that she had a vocation to save her people:

"Who knows? Perhaps you have come to royal dignity for just such a time as this," Mordecai tells her.[228] In *Woman of the Inner Sea* Uncle Frank points out to Kate that she too has a calling, to be the Queen of Sorrows. In a barren city, it is the woman of the inner sea, the one who has found a life-giving stream within herself, who is "appointed to contribute so often the mute rain with her own unbidden tears".[229] Her calling is to cry for herself and for those who, like her murdered children, are mute, unable to speak against the injustices they have suffered. Her unbidden tears will bring a measure of cleansing to a poisoned city that cannot speak the truth.

Kate has learned much during her time in exile that will help her survive in Sydney and fulfil her vocation. Like Esther, she has gained wisdom. As Fromberg Schaeffer notes,

> When Kate returns to Sydney she has learned what she needs to know: that suffering is in the nature of things; that the worst catastrophe that can occur is simply one among many; and that no crisis, however enormous, justifies expending everything on it.[230]

Kate can also judge between good and evil. She can see her Uncle Frank for what he really is. Though she still loves him dearly, "she came to appreciate in her stupor that though he was a saint he had a profoundly criminal soul."[231] It was painful for her to observe Uncle Frank's "drift in judgment",[232] his complete lack of any sense of wrongdoing in his criminal activities.

By returning Kate brings cleansing to the city, but she also receives something in return. In exile she had told her story of what happened on the fateful night. But on her return she learns the full story of what happened. The house fire had been deliberately lit by others who had, in fact, tried to kill her. Her estranged husband, Paul, was behind these activities. Learning this, Kate is able to let slip the great burden of her guilt. This brings her further reconciliation with herself and with others. She starts thinking of her mother "in an unlikely, intimate way she thought she had sworn off for life; in a way Kate's guilt for the lost children had until recently invalidated her."[233]

For Kate the passing of the burden of guilt also brings "the black onus of punishing Paul Kozinsky."[234] In this task she finds unexpected and timely assistance, almost divine help.

> Angels...descended from Canberra and Macquarie Street to take over the punishing of Paul Kozinski.[235]

Like Uncle Frank, Paul's illegal activities have finally caught up with him and he is arrested. As in *Esther*, the final section of this story offers a very "fast moving sequence of retribution and cleansing".[236] Retribution may have been slow in coming, but in the end it comes very swiftly. In quick succession Uncle Frank is convicted, Paul is arrested and Paul and his father are imprisoned. In the loss of her children Kate has been divested of what she treasured most. Balancing her massive loss, Paul is now divested of everything he treasures. Not only is he imprisoned, but his house is repossessed by the bank and, through the cunning of Kate, he loses the woman he loves.

In this story, as in the book of *Esther*, retribution is metered out to the wicked. In its emphasis on retribution *Woman of the Inner Sea* contains a warning for the present inhabitants of Sydney who feel that the way to prosper in their land of exile is through covert illegal activities.

An Australian literary spirituality of exile

In our study of the biblical texts we saw how Queen Esther had to muster all of her personal resources and transcend herself in order to avert the tragedy that threatened the Jewish people. When *Woman of the Inner Sea* begins, the unspeakable tragedy has already happened. The hero, Kate, has to muster all of her personal resources not to avert the tragedy but to survive it. Faced with such a massive loss, and weighed down by a huge burden of guilt, survival is already a self-transcending activity. Her flight to the outback was an attempt to keep living. As she told her friend, Murray, "either I do this or I shoot myself."[237]

Kate's situation is very similar to that of the first wave of Jewish exiles to Babylon. As her life had been shattered by the deaths of her children, so were the Jews distraught and traumatised by the bitter loss of Temple, monarchy and homeland. Above all, Kate and the first Jewish exiles were devastated by the felt loss of connection with the Sacred, whether experienced as God or as some inner grounding force. In such wretched situations survival is truly a self-transcending activity.

Similar comments can be made about *Cloudstreet*. The families in that story also face great and continuing losses, and they feel cut off from the Sacred. They, and the house in which they live, carry the guilt and pain of past events. They are tempted to run away from the suffering, and some of the characters occasionally do. Simply staying in the house, staying with the guilt and the pain, is a self-transcending activity.

To survive the massive trauma of exile is already an achievement. With the passage of time survival becomes more sure and a new phase begins – a phase of growth. We saw this with the Jewish exiles and we see it again in the Australian novels.

To some degree this growth and healing happens imperceptibly. The people and township of Myambah, even a terrible flood, bring a measure of healing to Kate, enabling her to journey deeper into the interior. The characters in *Cloudstreet* gradually experience healing, love, forgiveness and belonging simply by staying in their community.

Grace, the hidden, unexpected and free activity of God, also plays a role in this healing process. In *Woman of the Inner Sea*, Chiffley, the kangaroo, is a god-figure who journeys with Kate into the interior. Though concealed, God has not abandoned her. God is gently and faithfully leading Kate to her own inner sea. Towards the end of the story Chiffley saves Kate by striking a blow to the mid-section of the wicked Burnside, the man who caused the fire that destroyed her children. This action inevitably leads to Chiffley's being put down. Like Christ on the cross, Chiffley dies to save Kate. In *Cloudstreet*, also, there are a number of God figures – the Aboriginal, the brain-damaged Fish, even a pig that speaks in tongues – who watch over the characters and help to keep them together.

As with the biblical stories, human initiative is also important. *In Woman of the Inner Sea* Kate must speak, must express the pain of past events to another, to enable her healing to continue. Somehow, the hard work of the Lamb family in *Cloudstreet* contributes to keeping the characters together.

The painful situations experienced in both stories demands honesty from the characters. The Lamb family in *Cloudstreet* honestly acknowledge the painful truth that they feel abandoned by God. *In Woman of the Inner Sea* Kate must honestly tell her story. The tragedies they face do not allow the characters in either story to be consoled by the comfortable beliefs they previously held.

Faced with the tragedies of life, the characters in both stories find limited help in their Christian Churches which carry their own woundedness. Faced with the inadequacies of the institutional Church, the narrator of *Woman of the Inner Sea* argues that people must look to their own inner resources to survive. Their lives should be characterised by honesty and integrity. The author of *Cloudstreet* offers a different solution. While traditional images of God may not work, there is Something out there. Reality is sacred, spirit-filled. People have to be shown how to see this. The Aboriginal people can guide the newcomers to see the Sacred in a different way in the land of their exile, a way that will not necessarily be incompatible with their Christian heritage.

Our study of the biblical texts revealed a variety of responses to the experience of exile. The Australian novels we have studied also reveal a remarkable variety of response.

Woman of the Inner Sea is an east coast novel set in Sydney and moving in a north-westerly direction towards the centre of the continent. *Cloudstreet* is a west coast novel set in Perth and stubbornly refusing to move from that city. The vast geographic distance between the settings of the stories mirrors the distance between their two outlooks.

This difference of outlook certainly flows out of the nature of the cities involved. Sydney is an international city with a strong European character and a relatively small Aboriginal presence. It is not surprising that such a city would produce a novel with a strong emphasis on the fate and responsibilities of the individual. While having many international and European character-istics, Perth retains a much stronger Aboriginal presence. It is more isolated from the rest of the world than Sydney; indeed, it is geographically isolated from the bulk of Australia's population. It is also a much smaller city than Sydney. Its size, isolation and Aboriginal presence make it a more suitable setting for a story that promotes the community over the individual.

The narrator of *Cloudstreet* sees the city of Perth as spirit-filled and is opposed to the commonly held belief that one must journey to the interior of the continent to find the Sacred. A fundamental aspect of the psyche of white Australians is that they don't like to travel away from the coast, or at least away from rivers. Far from denigrating this fact, the narrator sees a spiritual signif-icance in it. In staying near to water, Australians are subconsciously responding to its living spirit, to its sacredness.

The narrator of *Woman of the Inner Sea* opts for the alternative position. One must journey away from the poisoned coastal city to find salvation. For the narrator, the physical journey to the interior facilitates the more essential inner journey producing healing for the person. The person must, however, return to the coastal city to bring a measure of healing and cleansing to it. People in exile have their vocations. In responding to their call, they find home for themselves and others.

The spiritual quest in *Cloudstreet* is extroverted, outward looking. The characters are urged to see the Sacred all around them. But this outward looking spirituality does have an inner dimension. Responding the Sacred around them, the characters discover soft parts, love really, within themselves. The spiritual quest in *Woman of the Inner Sea* is introverted. The goal is to find a life-giving sea within oneself that will help one survive the tragedies of life in exile. It is the inner, sacred dimension that is honoured though this too is nurtured by outward events and in turn benefits the community.

Both stories highlight the importance of community and solitude for people in exile. *Cloudstreet* resolves the tension between these two realities by giving the community precedence over solitude. Solitude has value for a time, but ultimately it is in the community that love, healing and forgiveness are to be found. *Woman of the Inner Sea* resolves the tension in favour of solitude. The effects of community can be both positive and negative. The surest way to survive is to find within oneself, through solitude, a font of living water that will enable one to survive the tragedies of life and the sins of the community.

As with the biblical stories, banqueting plays an important role in the community of Cloudstreet. The division between the Lambs and the Pickles lessens when the Lambs invite the Pickles to share with them a feast of prawns.[238] It is while the two families are having a meal beside the water that they are finally able to let Fish Lamb return to the water that beckons him. They are finally able to let him go.[239] In this story, as in the biblical stories, meals have empowering and community forming qualities for exiles.

Cloudstreet is a gut centred, experiential, anti-intellectual novel. The characters gain awareness in an instinctive way rather than through understanding. They do not know what will happen next and the story meanders like a river. This is often how exiles have to live. Lacking knowledge and clear direction, they have to battle on as best they can trusting only their instincts. The message of *Cloudstreet* is that if people can stay together as a community and keep battling, they will eventually come to believe and belong in Australia.

In contrast to the meandering character of *Cloudstreet*, *Woman of the Inner Sea* is a suspenseful tale in which everything happens for a purpose. To survive, and find God in the land of their exile, people must value the resources of their minds and imaginations as they value their senses and instincts.

Neither story envisages a return of white Australians to Europe. It is possible for them to belong in the land of their exile, stresses the narrator of *Cloudstreet*. The land loves them, and calls on them to remain. It is already their home, if only they can see it. The narrator emphasises the deep connectedness of all reality. He has no concerns about people of different races and cultures mixing together, intermarrying and learning from one another. He is convinced that all are one. As Quick realises, in the end "it's us and us and us."[241] Quick even sees little difference between himself and murderers: "Only difference is, they did things you and me just thought about."[242] In this story about community and reconciliation, differences between people gradually lose their importance.

The narrator of *Woman of the Inner Sea* believes that there are significant differences between people. In his story there are good people and bad people, and a few, like the not-so-Reverend Uncle Frank, who are half and half. In this story there is no reconciliation of enemies, and the wicked don't change their ways. One needs to be wary of evil people. The narrator also highlights the complexities of relationships between exiles from different parts of the world. A marital union and the birth of a child unites the families in *Cloudstreet*. The marriage of Kate and Paul in *Woman of the Inner Sea*, and the births of their children, produce no such happy consequences for their families who remain at logger-heads throughout the story. While not contemplating a return of white Australians to Europe, the narrator is aware of the existential difficulties of living in a multi-cultural community of exiles.

Finally, like the books of *Tobit* and *Esther*, *Cloudstreet* and *Woman of the Inner Sea* emphasise that speech and story telling are very important exile activities. It is through talking with one another that people come to see the deep connectedness of all reality, and discover the love within them, notes the narrator of *Cloudstreet*. For the narrator of *Woman of the Inner Sea*, freedom, salvation, and an end to self-alienation come when people truthfully tell, and own, their stories.

Conclusion

Locating an experience of exile

In this final chapter I will offer an interpretation of the texts that we have studied. My concern to date has been with a critical study of these texts to ascertain what they are saying about the experience of exile and the spirituality that flows from it.

Interpretation always has a subjective element. Understanding, which is the final objective of interpretation, entails a "fusing of horizons" in which the reader allows his or her world horizon to be fused with the horizon of the world projected by the text, creating a new transformed reality.[243] This fusing of horizons entails a willingness on the part of the reader to surrender to the aesthetic experience of the text by entering fully into the world it projects. But it also entails a critical engagement with the text in the light of one's faith, learning and life experience.

I will, therefore, bring my world view to the task of interpreting these texts, and this final section will have a necessarily subjective element. But I hope that my interpretation will be helpful for readers trying to interpret these texts in the light of their own experience.

I begin by asking: wherein can I locate my personal experience of exile? My first response is that it does not lie in a sense of exile from the land. Like many Australians, I love the land in which I live. I have always had sacred places: a branch high up in a tree where as a child I spent many hours just sitting, feeling peaceful and connected; a retreat centre at Douglas Park, near Sydney, whose deep gorges and cliffs carved out by the Nepean river are full of wonder and mystery; a slow ferry ride on Sydney Harbour which has always brought soothing and healing to a stressful life. I find it hard to share the feelings of alienation from the land experienced by the Lamb family in the early part of *Cloudstreet.*

While I have a sense of the sacredness of the land, I realise that the Aboriginal people can help me to deepen this appreciation. Many white Australians like the land but fail to see its sacredness, and their deep connection with it. Australian Catholic newspapers are often filled with advertisements encouraging people to make pilgrimages to sacred sites in Europe – Lourdes, Fatima, Knock, etc. The inference is that if you want to encounter the Sacred you must board a plane and fly to Europe. While respecting the sacredness of many places in Europe, I believe non-Aboriginal Australians need to learn from the Aboriginal people to see the Sacred in the land in which they live.

I do not wish to fall into the trap of romanticism about the land. It is often tough and harsh. It is also suffering from what people have done to it. But the land also rewards and heals. Our connection with the land works both ways. As *Cloudstreet* correctly stresses, the need is to be in relationship with the land, to respect it and to work with it. Ways also need to be found to give back to the land some of what has been taken from it.

I also like the claim of *Cloudstreet* that one does not have to journey to the interior of the continent to experience the Sacred in the land. The coastal areas of the country are also spirit-filled. In wanting to be near the coast and rivers, white Australians are responding to the spirit-filled character of water. This sacramental aspect of water has rich resonances in the Christian tradition.

A healthy relationship with the land also demands that the majority of people live in the more coastal regions of the continent where the land is able to sustain greater populations. It would be an abuse of the land if large numbers of people were to move to the interior. If my sense of exile does not lie in an alienation from the land, wherein does it lie?

I gained some insight through the historical research I undertook for this study. In *The Fatal Shore*, Robert Hughes speaks of the "convict stain", a sense of shame white Australians have carried as a result of the nation's beginnings as a penal colony. In the nineteenth century:

> the Stain would not go away: the late nineteenth century was a flourishing time for biological determinism, for notions of purity of race and stock, and few respectable native born Australians had the confidence not to quail when real Englishmen spoke of their convict heritage.[244]

The Australian response to this stain was, firstly, not to talk about it. Until the 1960s Australian history books barely mentioned the penal origins of white settlement. Our study of *Cloudstreet* and *Woman of the Inner Sea* has highlighted the alienating effects of silence.

The second response was to see blood as a solvent for the birth stain. In the Boer War and subsequent world wars thousands upon thousands of Australians were sent off to fight in Britain's wars in an attempt to atone for their country's shameful past, to prove they were not as bad as people might think. A "cultural cringe", a sense of anxiety about their worth, persisted in white Australians until well beyond the Second World War.[245] The arts have played an important role in healing this cultural cringe. Writers like Thomas Keneally and Tim Winton have been significant in the celebration of Australian culture, and in critical comment on it.

A further exiling factor for Australians was that for many years education was, in the words of Thomas Keneally, "education for alienation". As a consequence of British colonialism,

> All the books we read were full of trees we had never seen, most of our schooling was about places we knew nothing of and had never seen. We were actually educated to be exiles.[246]

Reflecting on Keneally's comments, Peter Quartermaine has written: "Such an education was subtly cruel and its effects likely to be lasting."[247]

The fall of Singapore to the Japanese in 1942 marked the beginning of the end of British cultural imperialism in Australia. But the Second World War also opened Australia to the increasing cultural, economic and military influence of the United States.[248] Massive post-war migration to Australia, firstly from Europe and more recently from Asia has brought further changes to the nation's character. These overarching cultural shifts have impacted Australia's "tender sense of national identity and purpose"[249] making it even harder for exiles to feel at home.

All of these factors, the birth stain and consequent cultural cringe, an education for alienation, and the effects of cultural shifts on a tender national identity, have contributed to the sense of exile that I, and many Australians, experience. None of these, however, sufficiently explain my personal experience of exile.

The centrality of the God question

My study of the biblical texts and the two Australian novels has helped me to appreciate the centrality of the God question for people in exile.

The initial experience of exile is invariably one of great loss. People in exile cannot be likened to questers who freely choose to embark on a journey of discovery, who leave their homelands in search of adventure, romance, excitement or whatever. The quester looks forward while exiles always look back to what was taken from them. Nor can people in exile be compared with pilgrims who have embarked on a conscious journey to God, a journey in which they seek self-improvement and change. Far from being a journey to God, exile is often experienced as a journey away from all that is valued, including God. People in exile are bitter and hurt from the experience and often, like the Jewish exiles in Babylon and the Lamb family in *Cloudstreet,* feel that they have been abandoned by God.

I believe something like this may have happened to the people exiled in Australia. Their response was silence. They decided not to talk about God, to live and act as if God does not exist, or at least, that God does not matter. As Frank Fletcher has noted, today "the *ethos* of Australia could be the most secular in the world."[249] In Australia, "apathy towards and suspicion of commitment to religious faith has become atradition."[250] I suspect that at the base of this apathy is a wail, a great overwhelming grief in a God who seems to have abandoned them.

Of course, not all Australians are irreligious. Like many others, I was raised in the Christian tradition of my forebears. I did, in fact, receive the legacy of two major Christian traditions, Irish Catholic from my father and evangelical Scottish Presbyterian from my mother. Though raised in the Catholic tradition, I certainly imbibed the sentiments of both. I am grateful for both religious traditions which have been a rich source of spiritual nourishment for me.

But I must acknowledge also the limitations of my religious tradition in revealing the saving presence God in Australia. As Philip Sheldrake has noted, until recent times this tradition:

> had a detached, a priori approach to doctrine [which] gave birth to a similarly structured theory of the spiritual life which was separated from the core of human experience and consequently was largely alienated from, for example, nature, the body and the feminine.[252]

Such an a priori religion, detached from experience, had the advantage that it could be transported with the convicts and planted unchanged on Australian soil. Its great weakness was its failure to take sufficient cognisance of the particular experience of Australians, including exile, and its consequent failure to adapt to the changing situation of life in the Australian continent.

Our study of the stories of *Tobit* and *Esther* has shown that exile is always a time for the translation, or reformulation, of religious belief in the light of new circumstances. With the collapse of the Monarchy, the destruction of the Temple in Jerusalem and the experience of exile, the Jewish people were forced to re-evaluate every aspect of their religion and their relationship with God. In our study of *Tobit* and *Esther*, we saw how the Jews used stories to help them in this reformulation of belief. We also saw how they took non-Jewish celebrations, such as the feast of Purim, and transformed them into Jewish celebrations.

Such a reformulation of belief in the light of new circumstances needs to continue to happen for the Australian exiles. In *Cloudstreet* we find the suggestion of a direction non-Aboriginal Australians can take in their efforts to translate the Christian faith. They have, in many of the Aboriginal people, wise guides who can help them to see the Sacred in the land. People in exile often experience an absent God. But as the texts we have studied have shown, God's presence may be concealed from our sight but God is not absent. Like Tobit, we need the help of others to heal our blindness.

To acknowledge the wisdom of the Aboriginal peoples is not to advocate that Christians reject their heritage and adopt Aboriginal religious customs, nor is it to suggest that at the base there is no difference between Aboriginal and Christian religions. The richest treasure the Jews took with them into exile was their religious heritage. It sustained them and gave them identity in a most critical time. It helped them to survive. Help also exists for Australian Christians in their religious tradition. But, as we saw in the book of *Esther*, religious traditions can be enriched through contact with the beliefs and culture of a different group of people. A broadening of vision will always be a positive consequence of exile.

A reformulation of religious belief in the light of new circumstances always takes time. We need to appreciate that the Babylonian exile occurred in 587 BCE, that the book of *Esther* was possibly written some two hundred years later, and that another two hundred years passed before it was accepted by Jews in Palestine. In Australia we are in the infancy of the reformulation stage. But reformulate we must because, as we have seen in all four texts we studied, the primary question raised by exile is always the question of where is God? An answer to that question is essential before people can feel at home in the land of their exile.

Woman of the Inner Sea suggests another important direction Australians must take in their search for God, a journey inwards to the depths of their being. The narrator believes that Australians focus too greatly on the surface matters of life. "Australia is periphery," he claims. "It dreams of and yet abandons the core."[253] Frank Fletcher has written about "the disinclination towards inwardness, the Australian preoccupation with the surface of life."[254] The poor wretches who constituted the original penal colony mostly focused on what outward things they could acquire or enjoy in the land of their exile. *Woman of the Inner Sea* suggests that this consciousness continues in many of the current inhabitants of Sydney. And, as the narrator suggests, newer immigrants seem to pick up the spirit of materialism very quickly.

This dominant consciousness which fears and resists all inwardness is also expressed in the struggle of Kate to journey to the interior of the continent. She is actually forced by tragic circumstances to move ever deeper into the interior. Going to the interior is risky because, as Australians know, either "answers or nullities could be found."[256] The great fear is that it will be the latter. But as *Women of the Inner Sea* reveals, people like Kate who have the courage to journey to the interior will find a sea of life-giving water. Ewert Cousins has expressed well the importance of this inner journey to one's spiritual core:

> it is here that the person is open to the transcendent dimension, it is here that the person experiences ultimate reality.[257]

As Aboriginal people can guide others to see the Sacred around them, so also Australians need helpers and guides on their journey to their deepest selves, helpers who are trustworthy and wise and reflective. Kate Gaffney-Kozinsky could never have made it to the interior on her own. But she could with the help of Jelly and Gus, and the totemic Chiffley. The quest for God in Australia needs to be both outward looking and inward looking. The ratio will, however, vary according to peoples' personalities and experiences. Likewise there will be diversity in the ritual expression of peoples' experience of God. Our study of the biblical texts has shown that the experience of exile can produce a remarkable diversity of response. In *Tobit* we saw the more conservative response of the Post-Deuteronomic reform which continued to look to a restored Jerusalem and the Temple as the place of the presence of God. *Esther* displayed no such interest in Jerusalem, boldly asserting that the land of exile is also the place of the saving presence of God. In time, even this radical response of *Esther* was accepted into the Hebrew and Christian Canons of Scripture. As we observe the variety of responses to exile in the Bible, I believe we are also called to a tolerance of different expressions of spirituality within Australia. As there is no single model of the exile, so there can be no one model of exile spirituality.

The importance of community and solitude

While Tobias, Kate and Quick, returned to their exile communities, and while individuals in some of the stories experienced a return to personal wholeness, in none of the stories did the exiled community itself return to the place from which it was exiled. *Tobit* is the only story to even envisage a future return of the exiles to their homeland. The clear message of the other stories is that there is no return of the community from exile.

Exiles are destined to remain for a long time in their place of exile, until some other set of circumstances pushes them into a new exile. Loss follows loss, as Kate Gaffney-Kozinsky discovered.

History has also shown that returns from exile are rare, and even more rarely successful. As the Jews who returned to Israel with the fall of the Babylonian empire discovered, return and restoration are very difficult. Returning exiles quickly find that the community from which they were exiled has changed in their absence, and that they too have changed. The former reality is lost forever.

Our study has, however, revealed the importance of community for people in exile. This community may be a family, or a couple of families, or it may be a race of people. Whatever its size, it is very important for people in exile to belong to a community. As the biblical stories stress, the survival of exiles is dependent on it.

The two Australian novels highlight the modern angst involved in living in community. It is a place of pain and guilt and sin. It is very difficult to remain within it. In *Cloudstreet* Quick fled the house unable to cope with the daily reminders of suffering and the guilt he felt every time he saw his brother, Fish. It is also a sense of guilt that isolated Oriel from her son, Fish, and forced her to physically vacate the house. In *Woman of the Inner Sea* Kate is also forced to flee Sydney because of guilt over her children's death, and because the community had alienated her from herself.

As I read the stories of Quick and Kate I recognise that I am reading my own story. In recent years I, too, fled my community and lived for two and a half years in the United States. Unlike Quick and Kate, I was not forced to flee by guilt but, like them, I felt I had to escape to survive. I also felt somewhat alienated from my inner self. I had little idea of what was at the bottom of my wail.

Cloudstreet and *Woman of the Inner Sea* both affirm that time away from the community, a time of solitude, is valuable. It is sometimes wise to honour the feeling of "I've got to get away from here." Quick had no ambitions for his time away. But while he was away, "a strange thing begins."[258] Quick gradually came to see the interconnectedness of human beings with each other and with the land. It was an unexpected experience of enlightenment. He also came to realise how much he missed Cloudstreet. The community was precious to him despite the pain involved in belonging to it. And so he returned.

For Kate also, time away from Sydney proved very fruitful. Like Quick she had few ambitions for her time. She just wanted to be anonymous, to disappear by changing her shape, and to have some space for herself. But then, "a strange thing begins." Healing started to happen. In time Kate grew in wisdom and connected with the life giving stream in the depths of her being.

My journey somewhat mirrors Kate's. Like her, my primary need when I left Australia was simply for space. In my first six months overseas I had little interest in community involvement. My priority was simply time for myself and I spent many hours in "my cherished room," reading, relaxing and in some ways simply being.

"But then a strange thing begins." I found that imperceptibly I was becoming a part of a community that was bringing great healing to me. I also began to experience an awareness that I was in a place where it is safe to take the journey of discovering who I am in the depths of my

being. Like Kate I found that I had wonderful companions on this journey. It was not easy for me to take
this inward journey. But I had no choice. As with Kate,
circumstances were forcing me ever deeper into the
interior, towards the discovery and claiming of my own
life giving inner sea.

While Quick and Kate benefitted greatly from their
time away, both realised eventually that they must
return to their exile community. And so did I. Unlike
Quick, I did not return because I was "homesick as a
dog" though certain longings to return were present. I
had to return because I felt it was my necessary role, my
vocation. The words of the Aboriginal in *Cloudstreet*
spoke with increasing insistence: "You've got a home to
go to. Go there." His words spoke to me of duty, but also
of promise, that I would be enriched by going home and
this has proved to be the case. Returning home has
brought further healing and understanding for me, as it
did for Quick and Kate in the novels we have studied.

Like Quick and Kate I needed to return to receive the
gifts that my community can give. When Quick
returned to Cloudstreet he began to make sense of the
past and came to realise that his is a shared tragedy. All
of the family shared the guilt of Fish's accident. Quick
received consolation from his family, and experienced
forgiveness from Fish. It was only on her return that
Kate learned the full story of what happened to her
children and was able to let slip the burden of guilt.

Like the families in *Cloudstreet* and the inhabitants of
Sydney in *Woman of the Inner Sea*, exile communities are
often fragmented as individuals battle with guilt and
the griefs of life's losses. Members are isolated from
each other by tragedy, and plunged into a deeper
personal sense of exile. They fail to recognise that they

are participating in a communal experience of tragedy. In sharing their stories, they become aware of their shared experience and find community.

As much as anything, this study has taught me that people in exile need to talk. It is through talking that the inhabitants of Cloudstreet come to recognise the deep connections that exist between them, and the shared experience of tragedy in their lives. For Kate Gaffney-Kozinsky, the woman of the inner sea, salvation came when she could tell her story, in all its horribleness and guilt, to another person. Talking can be a hard and bitter vocation. But for people in exile it is a pathway to salvation. Words are an important means through which we can mediate healing for what, I now believe, is a primary source of many peoples' sense of exile, including my own – alienation from community.

In both novels women play major roles in the story's resolution, and they do so through talking. Women do seem to be able to share stories with a greater facility than men who have historically let might and power and military force do the talking for them. In powerless exile situations women often come to the fore, and save communities, because they have learned to talk with each other, and with the men in their lives.

My own vocation on my return has been connected with writing and talking, with finding words to express something of my own experience, and our shared experience as humans.

Tobit reminds us that talking with God is also important. Often the only prayer exiles can make is the bitter, questioning prayer of lament to a God who appears to have turned away. The encouragement of Tobit to his fellow exiles is to pray that prayer with all their heart.

And then a strange thing begins...

If we can remain in our shattered communities, while at the same time respecting our needs for solitude, and if we have the courage to talk with each other and with God, the land of exile can, in fact, become home. This is the clear message of *Esther* and *Cloudstreet*. "You've got a home to go to. Go there", says the Aboriginal, the bearer of more than forty thousand years of wisdom in the great south land of the Holy Spirit. It is also the message of the Christian tradition. As the author of *Ephesians* tells Christian converts:

> *You are no longer strangers or aliens, but you are citizens with the saints and also members of the household of God, built upon the foundation of the apostles and prophets, with Christ Jesus himself as the cornerstone. In him the whole structure is joined together and grows into a holy temple in the Lord; in whom you also are built together spiritually into a dwelling place for God.*[259]

Notes

1 Sandra M. Schneiders, "Spirituality as an Academic Discipline: Reflections from Experience." *Christian Spirituality Bulletin* 1 (Fall, 1993): 12.

2 Tim Winton, *Cloudstreet* (Ringwood: McPhee Gribble, 1991).

3 Robert L. Ross, review of *Cloudstreet*, by Tim Winton, in *World Literature Today* 67 (Summer, 1993): 671.

4 Thomas Keneally, *Woman of the Inner Sea* (London: Hodder and Stoughton, 1992).

5 Two versions of the book of *Esther* can be found in Bibles: the original Hebrew text and the later Greek text which contains 107 additional verses that greatly alter the story's theological focus. These additional verses are included with the Apocrypha. The object of study in this book is the Hebrew version of *Esther*.

6 *Esther* was probably composed in the eastern Diaspora, around Susa, during the latter part of the Persian era (400 BCE to 322 BCE), though some scholars do suggest a later date in the Greek period. The place of composition of *Tobit* is unknown but it comes from the Diaspora and was composed around 200 BCE to 170 BCE. For a more detailed discussion on the date and place of composition of these books, see: John Craghan, *Ester, Judith, Tobit, Jonah, Ruth*, vol. 16, *Old Testament Message* (Wilmington, Michael Glazier, 1982), 10-11 134-35; Demetrius Dumm, "Esther", and Irene Nowell, "Tobit" in *The New Jerome Biblical Commentary*, eds. Raymond E. Brown, Joseph A. Fitzmyer, Roland E. Murphy (Englewood Cliffs: Prentice Hall, 1990), 568, 576.

References to *Tobit* and *Esther* in this book are from the *Holy Bible: New Revised Standard Version With Apocrypha* (Nashville: Thomas Nelson, 1990).

The words *Tobit* and *Esther* are underlined when the reference is to the biblical books. When the words Tobit and Esther are not underlined the reference is to the principal characters in the stories.

7 Winton, *Cloudstreet*, 220.

8 Sandra M. Schneiders, *The Revelatory Text: Interpreting the New Testament as Sacred Scripture* (San Francisco: Harper San Francisco, 1991).

9 *Ibid*, 142.

10 Robert Alter, *The Art of Biblical Narrative* (New York: Basic Books, 1981), 3.

11 Sallie McFague, *Models of God: Theology for an Ecological, Nuclear Age* (Philadelphia: Fortress Press, 1987), 43.

12 Philip Sheldrake, *Spirituality and History: Questions of Interpretation and Method* (New York: Crossroad, 1992), 52.

13 Schneiders, *The Revelatory Text*, 175.

14 For a detailed discussion of the Bible as mediator of the revelatory encounter with God, see Schneiders, *The Revelatory Text*, 157-79.

15 Sheldrake, *Spirituality and History*, 32.

16 See Schneiders, "Spirituality as an Academic . . . ", 13; Bernard McGinn, "The Letter and the Spirit: Spirituality as an Academic Discipline," *Christian Spirituality Bulletin* 1 (Fall, 1993): 5-6.

17 *Ibid*, 13.

18 Joann Wolski Conn, "Introduction," in *Women's Spirituality: Resources for Christian Development* ed. Joann Wolski Conn (New York: Paulist, 1986), 3.

19 Schneiders, "Spirituality as an Academic . . .", 11.

[20] Ibid.

[21] Rowan Williams, The Wound of Knowledge: Christian Spirituality from the New Testament to St. John of the Cross (London: Darton, Longman and Todd, 1979), 2.

[22] Schneiders, "Spirituality as an Academic . . .," 11.

[23] Ibid, 14.

[24] Conn, Women's Spirituality, 3.

[25] Walter Principe, "Toward Defining Spirituality," Sciences Religieuses 12 (1983), 135-36.

Exiled to Babylon

[26] Norman K. Gottwald, The Hebrew Bible: A Socio-Literary Introduction (Philadelphia: Fortress Press, 1985), 425.

[27] Psalm 137:1.

[28] Lester L. Grabbe, Judaism from Cyrus to Hadrian, vol. 1, The Persian and Greek Periods (Minneapolis: Fortress Press, 1992), 121.

[29] 2 Kings 24:14; 25:12.

[30] Grabbe, Judaism from Cyrus to Hadrian, 122.

[31] 2 Kings 17:5-6. Cf, Gottwald, The Hebrew Bible, 420.

[32] Esther 2:6.

[33] Tobit 1:2.

[34] Tobit 3:15.

[35] Will Soll, "Misfortune and Exile in Tobit: The Juncture of a Fairy Tale Source and Deuteronomic Theology," Catholic Biblical Quarterly 51 (January, 1989): 225.

Where is God in all this?

[36] Foreword to Ralph W. Klein, Israel in Exile: A Theological Interpretation, Overtures to Biblical Theology Series, eds. Walter Brueggemann and John R. Donahue, (Philadelphia: Fortress Press, 1979), xii.

[37] Esther 2:2.

[38] Esther 1:12.

[39] Esther 2:10.

[40] Esther 5:4, 8.

[41] Tobit 5:18.

[42] Tobit 5:22.

[43] Tobit 12:11.

[44] Tobit 12:14.

[45] Sandra Beth Berg, "After the Exile: God and History in the Books of Chronicles and Esther," in The Divine Helmsman: Studies on God's Control of Human Events, Presented to Lou H. Silberman, eds. James L. Crenshaw and Samuel Sandmel (New York: Ktav Publishing House, Inc, 1980), 115.

[46] I will use the masculine pronoun when referring to the narrators of both stories. None of the many commentaries I read on these works suggest that the author/narrator of either story is a woman. While I do not rule out this possibility, especially in the case of Esther, I agree that the weight of evidence in the texts points to a male author/narrator.

[47] Irene Nowell, "The Narrator in the Book of Tobit," in Society of Biblical Literature 1988 Seminar Papers, ed. David J. Lull (Atlanta: Scholars Press, 1988), 28.

[48] Tobit 5:22.

[49] Tobit 3:11.

[50] Nowell, "Tobit," 570.

51 Some scholars do, in fact, argue that the angel in *Tobit* is a manifestation of God's presence among the people. Cf., Craghan, *Esther, Judith, Tobit, Jonah, Ruth*, 141.

52 *Esther* 9:5-16.

54 *Esther* 9:16.

55 *Esther* 3:13.

56 *Esther* 8:11.

57 *Tobit* 1:3.

58 *Tobit* 3:6.

59 *Tobit* 3:14.

60 *Tobit* 14:15.

61 Demetrius Dumm, "Esther," 578.

62 George W. E. Nickelsburg, "Tobit and Enoch: Distant Cousins with a Recognisable Resemblance," in *Society of Biblical Literature 1988 Seminar Papers*, ed. David J. Lull (Atlanta: Scholars Press, 1988), 60.

63 *Tobit* 5:10.

64 Sidnie Ann White, "Esther: A Feminine Model for Jewish Diaspora," in *Gender and Difference in Ancient Israel*, ed. Peggy L. Day (Minneapolis: Fortress Press, 1989), 164.

65 *Esther* 3:15.

66 *Esther* 1:4.

67 *Esther* 1:3; 2:16.

68 Nickelsburg, "Tobit and Enoch", 60.

What must the Jews do in exile?

69 Berg, "After the Exile," 118.

70 *Esther* 10:3.

71 *Esther* 2:20.

72 *Esther* 2:18.

73 White, "Esther: A Feminine Model," 167.

74 Andre LaCocque, *The Feminine Unconventional: Four Subversive Figures in Israel's Tradition*, Overtures to Biblical Theology Series, eds. Walter Brueggemann, John R Donahue, Elizabeth Struthers Malbon, Christopher Seitz (Minneapolis: Fortress Press, 1990), 80.

75 White, "Esther: A Feminine Model . . .," 173.

76 Ibid, 166-67. Women are also highly regarded in *Tobit* as persons capable of prayer (3:11-15), wage earning (2:11-12) and religious education (1:8 where Tobit mentions that his grandmother, Deborah, was the primary source of his religious instruction). Beverley Bow and George Nickelsburg have noted that Sarah's prayer in 3:11-15 is "wiser, less self centred" than Tobit's prayer which immediately preceeds it in 3:2-6. See Beverly Bow and George W. Nickelsburg, "Patriarchy with a Twist: Men and Women in Tobit," in *"Women Like This": New Perspectives on Jewish Women in the Greco-Roman World*, ed. Amy-Jill Levine (Atlanta: Scholars Press: 1991), 130.

77 *Tobit* 1:10-11. Cf. *Leviticus* 11; *Deuteronomy* 14:3-21.

78 *Tobit* 2:4-9. Cf. *Numbers* 19:11-13.

79 *Tobit* 4:12. Cf. *Genesis* 11:29.31; 25:20; 28:1-4; 29:15-30; *Deuteronomy* 7:3.

80 The *Book of Esther* was also written with prosperous, important Jews in mind,

namely Jews who had achieved prominent places in the Persian Court. It sought to remind these people of their obligations towards less privileged Jews by providing them "with models of how to behave in such circles, without compromising proper Jewish worship or religion." Grabbe, *Judaism from Cyrus to Hadrian*, 121.

[81] *Tobit* 12:9.

[82] *Tobit* 3:2-6; 11-15.

[83] Klein, *Israel in Exile*, 154.

[84] *Tobit* 8:5-8.

[85] *Tobit* 12:6.

How should the Jews relate to their gentile overlords?

[86] D. Daube, "The Last Two Chapters of Esther," *Jewish Quarterly Review* 37 (1946-47) 140, 146-47, quoted in Bruce William Jones, "Two Misconceptions about the Book of Esther," *Catholic Biblical Quarterly* 39 (1977): 172.

[87] *Tobit* 3:9.

[88] *Tobit* 2:21-23.

[89] *Esther* 3:8.

[90] Other reasons will be discussed in the next section.

[91] LaCocque, *The Feminine Unconventional*, 61.

[92] While parodying the excesses of the Persian court, and highlighting the fickleness of the Persian leadership, the narrator does seem to have an admiration for many things Persian. In 3:15, for instance, he seems to admire the efficiency of the Persian postal system!

[93] *Tobit* 1:13-14.

[94] Soll, "Misfortune and Exile in Tobit," 212-219.

[95] Nowell, "Tobit," 568.

[96] McCarthy, Carmel, and William Riley, *The Old Testament Short Story: Explorations into Narrative Spirituality*, Message of Biblical Spirituality Series, ed. Carolyn Osiek, No. 7 (Wilmington: Michael Glazier, 1986), 142.

[97] Roland E. Murphy, *The Tree of Life: An Exploration of Biblical Wisdom Literature*, Anchor Bible Reference Library (New York: Doubleday, 1990), 4.

[98] *Tobit* 4:12.

[99] *Tobit* 1:4-7.

[100] *Tobit* 13:3; See also 13:6.

[101] Craghan, *Esther Judith, Tobit, Jonah, Ruth*, 134.

[102] LaCocque, *The Feminine Unconventional*, 60.

Is a journey of return envisaged?

[103] See *Deuteronomy* 12:1-14; 16:6.

[104] *Tobit* 13:9.

[105] *Tobit* 13:10.

[106] *Tobit* 14:6, 7.

[107] Berg, "After the Exile," 114.

[108] *Esther* 3:8, 12-14; 8:9-13; 9:2-3, 12, 16, 20-23, 27-31.

[109] S. D. Goitein, *Iyyunim ba-Mikra*, Studies in Scripture (Tel Aviv: Yavneh Press, 1957), 59; quoted in LaCocque, *The Feminine Unconventional*, 63.

A biblical spirituality of exile

[110] *Tobit* 1:18-19.

[111] Craghan, *Esther, Judith, Tobit, Jonah, Ruth*, 147.

[112] Nowell, "Tobit," 570.

[113] *Tobit* 6:3.

[114] Michael V Fox, *Character and Ideology in the Book of Esther*, Studies of Personalities of the Old Testament Series, ed. James L. Crenshaw (Colombia: University of South Carolina Press, 1991), 147.

[115] Brueggemann and Donahue, Foreword to Klein, *Israel in Exile*, xii.

[116] *Tobit* 4:1.

[117] *Tobit* 8:2.

[118] Klein, *Israel in Exile*, 151.

[119] Craghan, *Esther, Judith, Tobit, Jonah, Ruth*, 6.

[121] *Deuteronomy* 12:12; Also Deuteronomy 14:26; 16:11.

[122] Alter, *The Art of Biblical Narrative*, 34.

[123] Jones, "Two Misconceptions", 172.

Exiled to Australia

[124] Accusation made by Jeremy Bentham in 1812, criticising the establishment of the penal colony in Australia. Quoted in Robert Hughes, *The Fatal Shore: A History of the Transportation of Convicts to Australia, 1787-1868* (London: Collins Harvill, 1987), 2.

[125] *Ibid.*

[126] Manning Clark, *A Short History of Australia*, Third Revised Edition (New York: Mentor, 1963), 22.

[127] Hughes, *The Fatal Shore*, 44.

[128] *Ibid.* 2.

[129] W T Tyler, "Lighting Out For the Outback", *The Washington Post*, 28 February, 1993, 4 Book World.

[130] Max Harris and Alison Forbes. *The Land That Waited*, (Melbourne: Lansdowne Press, 1967), 4.

[131] Hughes, *The Fatal Shore*, xiii.

[132] In this study, the word *Cloudstreet* is underlined when the reference is to the book. Cloudstreet is not underlined when the reference is to the actual house in the story.

[133] Winton, *Cloudstreet*, 41.

[134] *Ibid.*

[135] *Ibid*, 231.

[135] Tyler, "Lighting Out for the Outback".

[136] Thomas Keneally, "Doing Research for Historical Novels," *The Australian Author* 7/1 (1975): 27; quoted in Peter Quartermain, *Thomas Keneally*, Modern Fiction Series, ed. Robin Gilmour, (London: Edward Arnold, 1991), 9.

Where is God in all this?

[137] Winton, *Cloudstreet*, 26.

[138] *Ibid*, 47.

[140] *Ibid.*

[141] Christina Thompson, "Tim Winton's Big River," *Scripsi* 7/3 (1991): 123.

[142] Winton, *Cloudstreet*, 368.

[143] *Ibid*, 362.

[144] *Ibid*, 406.

[145] *Ibid*, 25.

[146] *Ibid*, 211.

[147] *Ibid*, 218.

[148] *Ibid*, 300.

[149] *Ibid*, 217.

[150] *Ibid*.

[151] *Ibid*, 209.

[152] *Ibid*, 362.

[153] *John*, 13:4.

[154] *John*, 17:21.

[155] Winton, *Cloudstreet*, 333.

[156] *Ibid*, 396.

[157] *Ibid*, 415.

[158] Keneally, *Woman of the Inner Sea*, 11.

[159] *Ibid*, 233.

[160] *Ibid*, 58.

[161] *Ibid*, 116.

[162] *Ibid*, 111.

[163] *Ibid*, 118.

[164] *Ibid*, 95.

[165] *Ibid*, 96.

[166] *Ibid*, 125.

[167] *Ibid*, 143.

[168] *Ibid*, 212.

[169] *Ibid*, 212.

[170] *Ibid*, 214.

[171] *Ibid*, 218.

[173] Susan Fromberg Schaeffer, "The Woman Who Lost Her Children", *The New York Times Book Review*, 18 April 1993: 9.

[174] Keneally, *Woman of the Inner Sea*, 238.

[175] *Ibid*, 247.

[176] *Ibid*, 242.

What must people do in exile?

[177] Winton, *Cloudstreet*, 58.

[178] *Ibid*, 147.

[179] *Ibid*, 166.

[180] *Ibid*, 124.

[181] *Ibid*, 174.

[182] *Ibid*, 391-2.

[183] *Ibid*, 294.

[184] *Ibid*, 383.

[185] *Ibid*, 75, 92.

[186] *Ibid*, 62.

[187] *Ibid*, 405-6.

[188] *Ibid*, 402.

[189] *Ibid*, 134.

[190] *Ibid*, 406.

[191] *Ibid*, 60.

[192] *Ibid*, 407.

[193] Beth Watzke, "This Great Continent of a House," *Antipodes* 5/2 (December 1991): 147.

[194] Marion Halligan, "Shall We Gather at the River," *Australian Book Review*, No 129 (April 1991): 4.

[195] Winton, *Cloudstreet*, 179.

[196] *Ibid*, 183

[197] *Ibid*, 353.

[198] *Ibid*, 357.

[199] *Ibid*, 358

[200] *Ibid*, 359

[201] *Ibid*, 357.

[202] Published in the Australian and British editions of the book but not in the North American edition.

[203] Keneally, *Woman of the Inner Sea*, 221.

[204] Winton, *Cloudstreet*, 213.

[205] *Ibid*, 294.

[206] Keneally, *Woman of the Inner Sea*, 211. I have given the extended quote found in the revised North American edition of this book (New York: Nan A. Talese/Doubleday, 1993), 202.

[207] *Ibid*, 211.

[208] Fromberg Schaeffer, "The Woman Who Lost . . .," 9.

How should non-Aboriginal Australians relate to the Aboriginal people?

[209] Winton, *Cloudstreet*, 79.

[210] *Ibid*, 8.

[211] *Ibid*, 15.

[212] *Ibid*, 411.

[213] *Ibid*, 14.

Is a journey of return envisaged?

[215] *ibid*, 368.

[216] *Ibid*, 141.

[217] *Ibid*, 419.

[218] *Ibid*, 31.

[219] *Ibid*.

[220] Bula Maddison, "The Spirit and the Anthropologist," 1993. TMs [photocopy], p. 14.

[221] Winton, *Cloudstreet*, 253.

[222] Keneally, *Woman of the Inner Sea*, 247.

[223] Claire Mills, review of *Woman of the Inner Sea* by Thomas Keneally, in *Australian Bookseller and Publisher* 71 (April 1992): 28.

[224] Keneally, *Woman of the Inner Sea*, 193.

[225] *Ibid*, 191.

[226] *Ibid*.

227 *Ibid*, 203.

228 *Esther:* 4:14.

229 Keneally, *Woman of the Inner Sea*, 12.

230 Fromberg Schaeffer, "The Woman Who Lost . . .," 9.

231 Keneally, *Woman of the Inner Sea*, 250.

232 *Ibid*, 270.

233 *Ibid*, 263.

234 *Ibid*, 273.

235 *Ibid*, 280.

236 D. R. Burns, "Confident Mastery," *Overland* 129 (Summer, 1992): 84.

An Australian literary spirituality of exile

237 Keneally, *Woman of the Inner Sea*, 76.

238 Winton, *Cloudstreet*, 273.

239 *Ibid*, 1-3.

241 Winton, *Cloudstreet*, 402.

242 *Ibid*.

Conclusion

243 Schneiders, *The Revelatory Text*, 172.

244 Hughes, *The Fatal Shore*, xii.

245 *Ibid*.

246 Laurie Clancy, "Thomas Keneally's Three Novels", *Meanjin* 112, XXVII, 1968, 37, quoted in Peter Quartermaine, *Thomas Keneally*, 4.

247 Quartermaine, *Thomas Keneally*, 4.

248 *Ibid*, 5.

249 *Ibid*.

249 Frank Fletcher, "Drink from the Well of Oz," in Peter Malone, ed., *Discovering an Australian Theology*, (Homebush: St Pauls Publications, 1988) 65.

250 *Ibid*.

252 Sheldrake, *Spirituality and History*, 33.

253 Keneally, *Woman of the Inner Sea*, 179.

254 Fletcher, "Drink from the Wells of Oz," 65.

256 Keneally, *Woman of the Inner Sea*, 78.

257 Cousins, "What is Christian Spirituality?", 40.

258 Winton, *Cloudstreet*, 204.

259 *Ephesians* 3:19-22.

Bibliography

Australian Studies:

Cameron, Rod. *Alcheringa: The Australian Experience of the Sacred.* Homebush: St Pauls, 1993.

Clark, Manning. *A Short History of Australia.* 3rd revised ed. New York: Mentor, 1987.

Edwards, Denis. *Called to Be Church in Australia: An Approach to the Renewal of Local Churches.* Homebush: St Paul Publications, 1989.

Harris, Max, and Alison Forbes. *The Land That Waited.* Melbourne: Lansdowne Press, 1967.

Hughes, Robert. *The Fatal Shore: A History of the Transportation of Convicts to Australia, 1787-1868.* London: Collins Harvill, 1987.

Kelly, Tony. *A New Imagining: Towards an Australian Spirituality.* Blackburn: Collins Dove, 1990.

Malone, Peter, ed. *Discovering an Australian Theology.* Homebush: St Paul Publications, 1988.

Tacey, David J., E*dge of the Sacred: Transformation in Australia.* North Blackburn: Harper Collins, 1995.

Thornhill, John. *Making Australia: Exploring Our National Conversation.* Newtown: Millenium Books, 1992.

Biblical Studies:

Alter, Robert. *The Art of Biblical Narrative.* New York: Basic Books, 1981.

Berg, Sandra Beth. *The Book of Esther: Motifs, Themes and Structure*, Society of Biblical Literature Dissertation Series, eds. Howard C. Kee and Douglas A. Knight, no. 44. Atlanta: Scholars Press, 1979.

Berg, Sandra Beth. "After the Exile: God and History in the Books of Chronicles and Esther." In *The Divine Helmsman: Studies on God's Control of Human Events, Presented to Lou H. Silberman*, eds. James L. Crenshaw and Samuel Sandmel, 107-27. New York: Ktav Publishing House, Inc., 1980.

Bow, Beverly, and George W. E. Nickelsburg. "Patriarchy with a Twist: Men and Women in Tobit." In *"Women Like This": New Perspectives on Jewish Women in the Greco-Roman World*, ed. Amy-Jill Levine, 127-143. Atlanta: Scholars Press, 1991.

Craghan, John. *Esther, Judith, Tobit, Jonah, Ruth*. Old Testament Message Series, eds. Carroll Stuhlmueller and Martin McNamara, vol. 16, Wilmington: Michael Glazier, 1982.

Davies, W. D., and Louis Finkelstein, eds. *The Cambridge History of Judaism*. Vol. 1, *Introduction; The Persian Period*. Cambridge: Cambridge University Press, 1984.

Dumm, Demetrius. "Esther." In *The New Jerome Biblical Commentary*, eds. Raymond E. Brown, Joseph A. Fitzmyer and Roland E. Murphy, 576-79. Englewood Cliffs: Prentice Hall, 1990.

Fox, Michael V. *Character and Ideology in the Book of Esther*, Studies of Personalities of the Old Testament Series, ed. James L. Crenshaw. Columbia: University of South Carolina Press, 1991.

Gottwald, Norman K. *The Hebrew Bible: A Socio-Literary Introduction*. Philadelphia: Fortress Press, 1985.

Grabbe, Lester L. *Judaism from Cyrus to Hadrian*, Vol. 1, *The Persian and Greek Periods*. Minneapolis: Fortress Press, 1992.

Jones, Bruce W. "Two Misconceptions About the Book of Esther," *Catholic Biblical Quarterly* 39 (1977): 171-81.

Klein, Ralph W. *Israel In Exile: A Theological Interpretation*, Overtures to Biblical Theology Series, eds. Walter Brueggemann and John R. Donahue. Philadelphia: Fortress Press, 1990.

LaCocque, Andre. *The Feminine Unconventional: Four Subversive Figures in Israel's Tradition.* Overtures to Biblical Theology Series, eds. Walter Brueggemann, John R. Donahue, Elizabeth Struthers Malbon, Christopher Seitz. Minneapolis: Fortress Press, 1990.

McCarthy, Carmel, and William Riley. *The Old Testament Short Story: Explorations into Narrative Spirituality.* Message of Biblical Spirituality Series, ed. Carolyn Osiek, no. 7. Wilmington: Michael Glazier, 1986.

McKenzie, Steven L., and Stephen R. Haynes, eds. *To Each Its Own Meaning: An Introduction to Biblical Criticisms and their Application.* Louisville: Westminster/John Knox Press, 1993.

Moore, Carey A. *Esther.* Anchor Bible Series, eds. William F. Albright and David D. Freedman, no. 7B. New York: Doubleday, 1971.

Moore, Carey A. "Scholarly Issues in the Book of Tobit Before Qumran and After: An Assessment," *Journal for the Study of the Pseudepigrapha* 5 (1989): 65-89.

Moore, Carey A. ed., *Studies in the Book of Esther.* New York: Ktav Publishing House, Inc, 1982.

Murphy, Roland E. *The Tree of Life: An Exploration of Biblical Wisdom Literature*, Anchor Bible Reference Library, ed. David N. Freedman. New York: Doubleday, 1990.

Nickelsburg, George W. E. "Tobit and Enoch: Distant Cousins with a Recognisable Resemblance." In *Society of Biblical Literature 1988 Seminar Papers*, ed. David J. Lull, 54-68. Atlanta: Scholars Press, 1988.

Nowell, Irene. "The Narrator in the Book of Tobit." In *Society of Biblical Literature 1988 Seminar Papers*, ed. David J. Lull, 27-38. Atlanta: Scholars Press, 1988.

Nowell, Irene. "Tobit." In *The New Jerome Biblical Commentary*, eds. Raymond E. Brown, Joseph A. Fitzmyer and Roland E. Murphy, 568-571. Englewood Cliffs: Prentice Hall, 1990.

Powell, Mark Allan. *What is Narrative Criticism*. Guides to Biblical Scholarship, New Testament Series, ed. Dan O. Via Jr. Minneapolis: Fortress Press, 1990.

Schneiders, Sandra M. *The Revelatory Text: Interpreting the New Testament as Sacred Scripture*. San Francisco: Harper San Francisco, 1991.

Soll, Will. "Misfortune and Exile in Tobit: The Juncture of a Fairy Tale Source and Deuteronomic Theology." *The Catholic Biblical Quarterly* 51 (January, 1989): 209-31.

White, Sidnie Ann. "Esther: A Feminine Model for Jewish Diaspora." In *Gender and Difference in Ancient Israel*, ed. Peggy L. Day, 161-77. Minneapolis: Fortress Press, 1989.

Spirituality and Theology (excluding Australian):

Borg, Marcus. *Meeting Jesus Again for the First Time: The Historical Jesus and the Heart of Contemporary Faith*. San Francisco: Harper San Francisco, 1994.

Conn, Joann Wolski, ed. *Women's Spirituality*. New York: Paulist, 1986.

Cousins, Ewert H. "What is Christian Spirituality?" In *Modern Christian Spirituality: Methodological and*

Historical Essays, ed. Bradley C. Hansen, 39-44. Atlanta: Scholars Press, 1990.

Edwards, Denis. *Human Experience of God*. With an Introduction by Avery Dulles. New York: Paulist, 1983.

McFague, Sallie. *Models of God: Theology for an Ecological Nuclear Age*. Philadelphia: Fortress Press, 1987.

McGinn, Bernard. "The Letter and the Spirit: Spirituality as an Academic Discipline." *Christian Spirituality Bulletin* 1 (Fall, 1993): 1-10.

Principe, Walter. "Toward Defining Spirituality," *Sciences Religieuses* 12 (1983): 135-36.

Schneiders, Sandra M. "Spirituality as an Academic Discipline: Reflections from Experience." *Christian Spirituality Bulletin* 1 (Fall, 1993): 10-15.

Schneiders, Sandra M. "Spirituality and the Academy", in *Modern Christian Spirituality: Methodological and Historical Essays*, ed. Bradley C. Hansen, 15-38. Atlanta: Scholars Press, 1990.

Sheldrake, Philip. *Spirituality and History: Questions of Interpretation and Method*. New York: Crossroad, 1992.

Literary Studies:

Jauss, Hans R., *Question and Answer: Forms of Dialogic Understanding*. Edited, Translated and with a Foreword by Michael Hays. Theory of History and Literature Series ed. by Wlad Godzich and Jochen Schulte-Sasse. Minneapolis: University of Minnesota Press, 1989.

O'Connor, Flannery, *Mystery and Manners: Original Prose, Selected and Edited by Sally and Robert Fitzgerald*. New York: Farrar, Strauss and Giroux, 1957.

Cloudstreet:

Anthony, Marilyn. Review of *Cloudstreet*, by Tim *Winton*. In Westerly 37 (Winter, 1992): 91-93.

Batstone, David. "Spinning Stories: Visions." *Sojourners* (October, 1992): 18-21.

Daniel, Helen. "Plotting 7, An Account of Some Recent Australian Fiction." *Overland* 123 (Winter, 1991): 72-77.

DeRossitt, James. Review of *Cloudstreet* by Tim Winton. In *Review of Contemporary Fiction* 12 (Fall, 1992): 200-01.

Forbes, Sandy. "With Love, From a Time When Life Was Simpler." *The Canberra Times*, 13 April 1991: (B)8.

Franklin, Carol. "Neighbours, Dreams and Neighbours." *Southerly* 51 (December, 1991): 152-63.

Halligan, Marion. "Shall We Gather at the River?" *Australian Book Review* 129 (April, 1991): 3-4.

Maddison, Bula. "The Spirit and the Anthropologist, 1993" TMs [photocopy].

Raines, G. "Recent Australian Prose." *Australian Studies (U.K.)* 6 (November, 1992): 145-51.

Ross, Robert L. Review of *Cloudstreet*, by Tim Winton. In *World Literature Today* 67 (Summer, 1993): 671.

Thompson, Christina. "Tim Winton's Big River." *Scripsi* 7/3 (1991): 119-124.

Watzke, Beth. "This Great Continent of a House..." *Antipodes* 5 (December, 1991): 147.

Webb, Benjamin S. "Tragedy and Redemption in Beloved Communities: The Role of Absence and Return, 1993" TMs [photocopy].

Winton, Tim. *Cloudstreet*. Minnesota: Graywolf Press, 1992.

Winton, Tim, and H. A. Willis. "According to Winton." *Eureka Street,* September, 1994, 20-25.

Woman of the Inner Sea:

Blanche, Cynthia. "Branded and Unbranded." *Quadrant* 37 (May, 1993): 80-82.

Brain, Robert. "Helping Out in the Outback." *Times Literary Supplement,* 26 June 1992, 20.

Burns, D. R. "Confident Mastery." *Overland* 129 (Summer 1992): 84-86.

Cameron, Deborah, "Swift Tom's Travels." *The Sydney Morning Herald,* 13 June 1992, 42.

Foster, Catherine. "Self-Discovery in the Australian Outback," *The Christian Science Monitor,* 7 April, 1993, 14.

Fromberg Schaeffer, Susan. "The Woman Who Lost Her Children." *The New York Times Book Review,* 18 April, 1993, 9.

Keneally, Thomas. *Woman of the Inner Sea.* London: Hodder and Stoughton, 1992; Plume Books, 1994.

Koenig, Rhoda. Review of *Woman of the Inner Sea* by Thomas Keneally. In *New York* 26 (15 March, 1993): 69.

Luke, Margot. "Famous For Something." *Australian Book Review* 141 (June, 1992): 10-11.

Mills, Claire. Review of *Woman of the Inner Sea* by Thomas Keneally. In *Australian Bookseller and Publisher* 71 (April, 1992): 28.

O'Hearn D. J. "Prolific Keneally Loves and Tells." *The Age Saturday Extra,* 20 June 1992: 9.

Quartermaine, Peter. *Thomas Keneally.* Modern Fiction Series, ed. Robin Gilmour. London: Edward Arnold, 1991.

Reimer, A. P. Review of *Woman of the Inner Sea* by Thomas Keneally. *The Sydney Morning Herald*, 13 June 1992, 42.

Sheppard, R. Z. "Deep in the Outback ." *Time* 141 (3 May 1993): 79-80.

Stead, C. K. "God's Gift to Australia." *London Review of Books* 14 (24 September, 1992): 20.

Tyler, W. T. "Lighting Out For the Outback." *The Washington Post*, 28 February, 1993, 4 Book World.